Telephones, Love Hearts & Jellyfish

Poèmes surréalistes [illegible] des boissons

First published in Great Britain 2

ISBN: 978 0 9568979 3 0
Author: Winston Plowes

Script:
© Winston Plowes 2015

Photography:
© Winston Plowes 2015 excluding those stated below.

Cover Photo: Wall of bottles at the Domaine Chandon Winery, Yountville, CA 94599 USA, by Dave Minogue 2008. Reproduced with permission.

Section 1: Glass Half Full
Page 5. Photograph of 'Glass Dragon' by Robin Parker. Reproduced with permission.

Section 3: Java Lounge
Pages 65-67 and 71, images by Ruth Robson-King. Reproduced with permission.

Section 5: Beer is Good
Page 76. Image from NASA, reproduced under Creative Commons Attribution 4.0 International Public License.
All other images in Section 5, pages 74-82 reproduced with permission by Pete Anderson, The Pareidolia Brewing Co, Sebastian, Florida USA.

Layout, design and typography:
© Electric Press

Also by Winston Plowes:
First Draught, Self Published (2008)
Misery Begins at Home, Jointly Self Published (2010)
Extras, Origami Poetry Press (2014)

Electric PRESS

Paper used in the production of this book is a natural, recyclable product made from wood grown in sustainable forests.

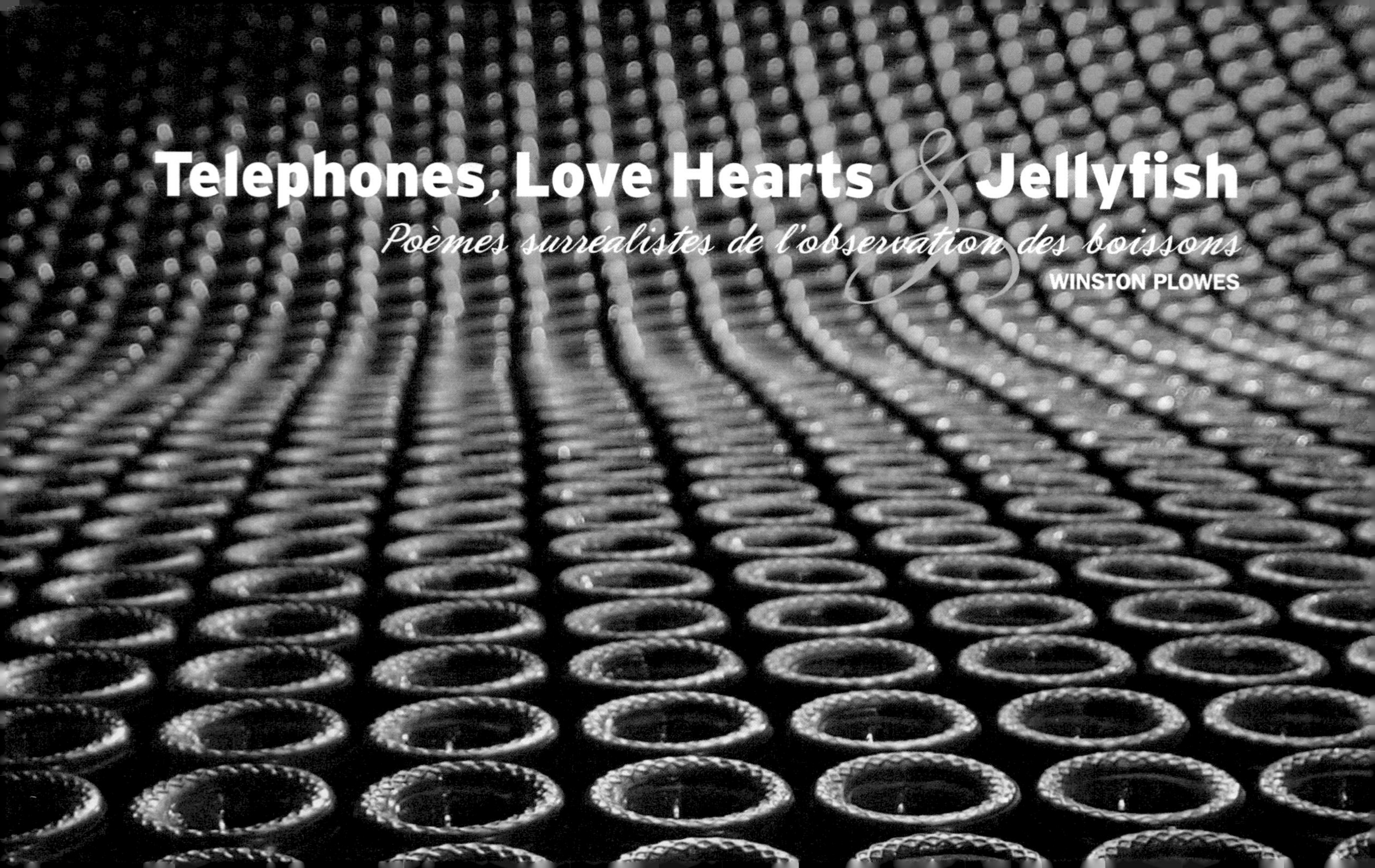
Telephones, Love Hearts & Jellyfish
Poèmes surréalistes de l'observation des boissons
WINSTON PLOWES

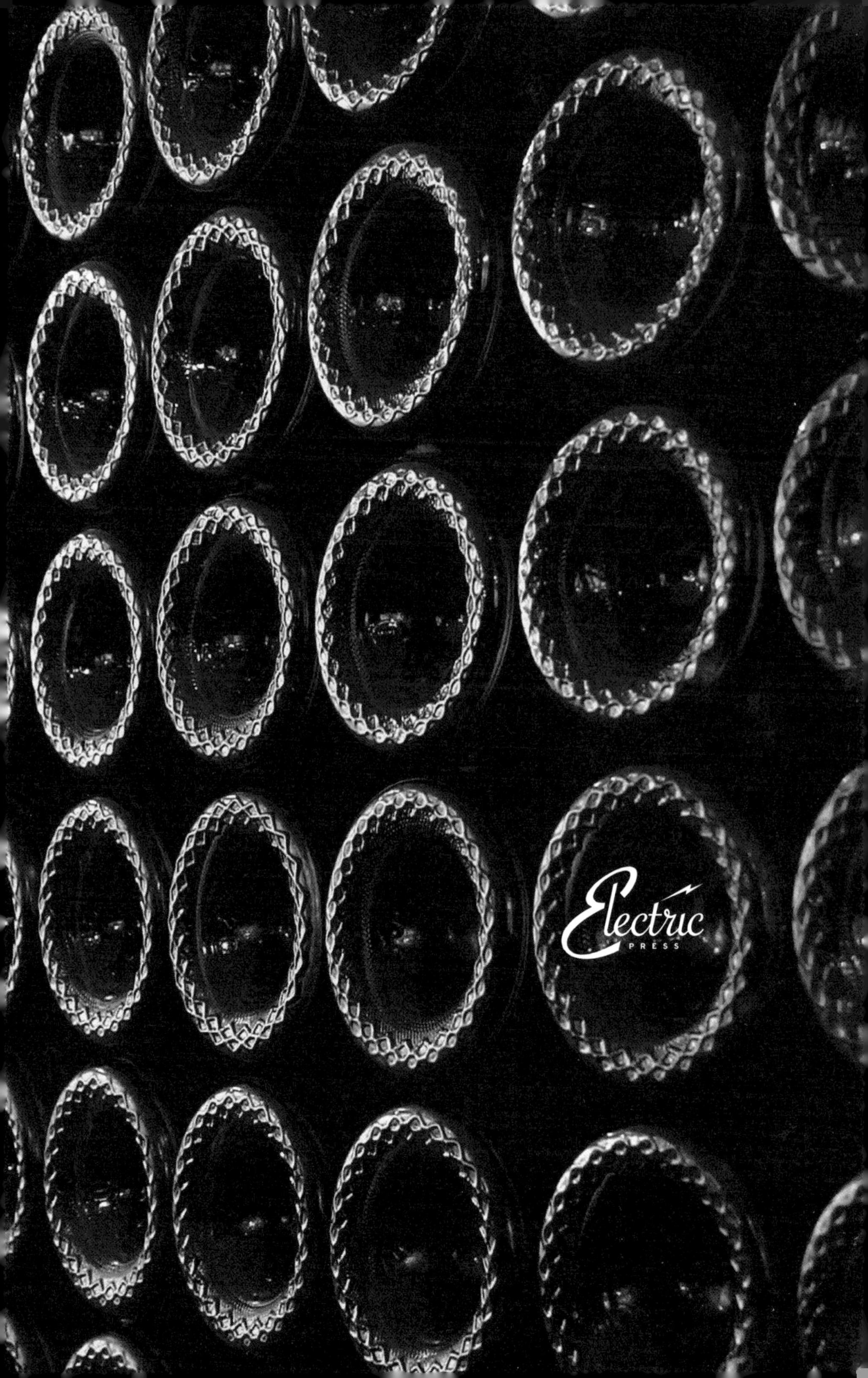
Electric
PRESS

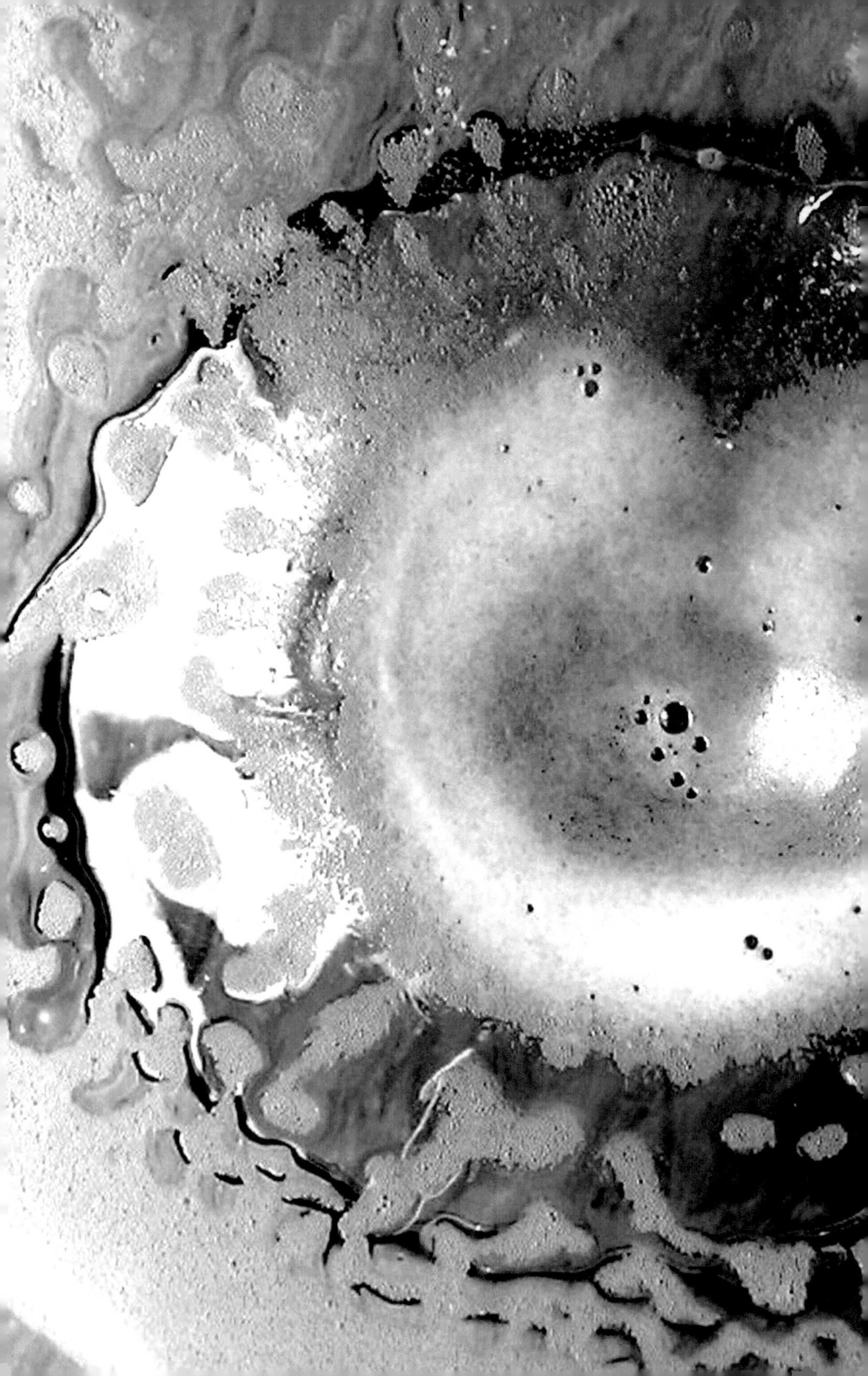

For a Poetess

"...beautiful
as the chance
meeting on a
dissecting-table,
of a sewing machine
and an umbrella."

Isidore Ducasse
(Comte de Lautréamont)
1846-1870

Contents

About This Book

Glass Half Full

Belgian Lace

Two Cats Kissing 6
Stone Skipping 7
Playing Football in the Style of Matisse 9
Top to Bottom 10
Telephone Chess 11
Piano Curling 12
Shark Fins 13
The Surprise Reappearance of New Zealand 14
Distant Rain Dance 15
May I Have the Next Dance 17
Tanks on the White House Lawn 18
The Scream 19
The Perforated Edge of Heaven 21
Bicycle Handlebars 22
Goat Wattles 23
Tintin et la Fusée Italienne 25
Jellyfish in Triplicate 26
Twitcher 27
Girl With the Wind in Her Hair 29
Pandas Versus Cows 31
The Mercator Projection of Endor 33
A Bask of Crocodiles 34
Oviposium 36

Park Life

The Coca-Cola Years

Bibendum 40
Scots Pine Distortions 41
Baily's Beads 42
The Flowers of Orion 43
Halva Moon 44
Picking the Cathedral's Locks 45
Random Inflations 46
F is for Teapot 47
Formation N°6 48
The Raised Eyebrow of Wilma Flintstone 49

The Green Room

A Chronology

The Thought Fox ... 52
Petroleum Kisses ... 53
The Last Flake of Snow on Middle Earth ... 54
A Crooked Smile on Mount Rushmore ... 55
Spiv Bomb ... 56
The White Rainbow ... 57

Java Lounge

In the Wake of the Wonderful Bean

Coppice on the Skyline ... 60
The Eye of a Whale ... 61
The Curious Incident of the Dog in the Night-Time ... 62
Shadows of Space ... 63
Three Wishes for The Hoff ... 64
Dogs Only Dream in Black and White ... 65
Pearls of the Night Boatman ... 66
Storm Door ... 67
Bent-kneed in Snow ... 68
Dot in the Distance ... 69
The Empathy Trap ... 70

Beer is Good

Chinking Glasses Across the Pond

Single Scoop Backdrop ... 74
Rabbit Unmasked ... 75
The Earth Was Born in a Pinball Machine ... 76
Leaning on the Spade ... 77
The Unexplored Face ... 78
Old Grey Mare ... 79
Names on an Unlikely Guest List ... 80
Under the Bark of Life ... 81
Hopeful Monsters ... 82

Monochrome Alternations

Two Men's Musings

Invasion of the Alien Bees 86
Floodlit Autopsy 87
Carnival of the Animals 88
Space Cowboy 89
Tales from the Land of Nod 90
Perseus Entombed 91
Je t'aime 92
The Rise and Fall of the Butterfly 93
Broken Trust 94
In a City Park 95

Sensory Miscellanea

of Oddly Shaped Treasures

A Perfect Square 98
Few Could Endure that Terrible Gaze 100
Teenage Mutation 101
Surface Tension 102
Reflections from a Torchlit Dream 103
Gift of Life 104
The Life of a Humpback Whale 105

Appendices

Cabinet of Curiosities 107
List of Beverages 118
List of Locations 119
Afore Ye Go 120

Collaborators' Biographies 122
Acknowledgements 123
Further Reading 124

Index 125

"The Rorschach of beverages, Winston Plowes – part tea leaf reader, part cloud namer – imaginatively finds multiple figures and story lines within glasses of beer and soda, within cups of coffee and tea. These list poems, written solo and collaboratively, bring wonder and humour to oft overlooked moments of everyday life."

Kelly Nelson
Poet & lecturer
Arizona State University

About This Book

WITHIN THESE PAGES you will discover kissing cats, a whale jumping out of the sea, sculptures by Henry Moore, and multiple appearances of telephones, love hearts and jellyfish. These are just some of the wonderful images discovered by the author and his collaborators in this book. The fruits of exhaustive research uncover the mysteries floating on the surfaces of beverages and clinging to the sides of their cups and glasses. An attempt to catalogue in the language of poetry, a phenomenon familiar to us all. I welcome you, the reader, to the surreal world of the poetry of drinks.

We often notice likenesses of objects or faces in cloud formations or in the knots of wood. They are all around us and can appear when least expected, inside a fruit when it's sliced open, amongst a jumble of scrap metal, on a piece of toast, or within the shadows of night.

Perhaps confusingly, there are at least five related terms (sometimes used synonymously) to describe this type of phenomenon.

Apophenia: An umbrella term used in psychology to describe the experience of seeing meaningful patterns or connections in random or meaningless data. The term was coined by neurologist Klaus Conrad in 1958, who added the definition, "*the unmotivated seeing of connections*".

Synchronicity: A related concept introduced by Carl Jung in the 1920's who believed that coincidental events with some symbolic significance were actually meaningful.

More specifically to imagery, and therefore more useful in this case, are the following terms:

Simulacrum: (plural, *simulacra*) A noun used to describe a slight, unreal, or vague semblance of something, a superficial likeness, a representation or imitation of a person or thing. Most commonly and originally this representation took the form of a statue or a painting, especially of a god, but broader applications of the term are now in use.

Patternicity: (or pattern-seeking) is a relatively recent term, coined in 2008 by Michael Shermer, who defined it as the tendency to find meaningful patterns in meaningless noise.

And finally…

Pareidolia: (*parr-i-DOH-lee-ə*) A type of apophenia in which some people are able to see vague or random images as something significant, typically shapes and faces.

So, is there something different about the way in which the brains of poets work that enables them to tune into these phenomena and see images more readily than most?

Some of the imagery in the poems here might seem to reveal something of the author, the minutiae of his accumulated knowledge, his sensibilities, or childhood experiences. Some of the lines may appear purely random, others may tell a vaguely connected story or have repeated or connected lines, whilst others still might just be an interesting collection of happenings. No editing or omissions have been made whilst composing these poems, and lines are transcribed in the order they presented themselves. Some lines are inspired by images from within the body of the drink concerned or from the patterns on its surface, others come from the sides or bottom of the glass. Some poems are a collection of interpretations from one instance in time whilst others are a progression as a drink is consumed, poured, stirred or swirled. Some images might linger just below the lip of a coffee cup whilst others appear only fleetingly in the rising bubbles of champagne.

Poems are categorised primarily by method of composition but also with chapters devoted to Glastonbury Festival, found coffee cups, craft beers from The Pareidolia Brewing Co. in Florida, and glasses of Coca-Cola drunk in a local cafe. I was very lucky to be able to crowd-source some of the entries via Facebook where so many imaginative friends posted their interpretative responses to my photographs. Where possible I have included photographs of the actual drinks alongside the poems they inspired, so that you can see the process for yourself and maybe even hone your own skills of observation. Where images seemed obscure or not common knowledge, I have annotated the poem and compiled an interesting and comprehensive list in the Appendix: *A Cabinet of Curiosities*.

For my hybrid style titles, in most cases I have chosen to combine actual *and* implied elements from the lines of each poem to compose something fitting.

We are dealing here with a relative of two of the Surrealist's favourite tools. Firstly, automatism (sometimes called free writing or automatic writing), where the writer is trying to allow unconscious thought processes to guide their hand across the page. In this case, influenced by the stimulus of patterns they see before them. Secondly, a version of the paranoiac-critical technique developed by Salvador Dali, in which multiple interpretations of an ambiguous image are represented in the same work, exploiting the brain's ability to perceive links between things which are not rationally linked.

We can find earlier records of pareidolia in writing. Da Vinci recorded in his notebooks how he saw landscapes and faces in cracked walls. Shakespeare gave us another example in *Hamlet*, where Polonius and Hamlet discuss the realism of animals they see in clouds, (*see page 105*).

In recording this menagerie of pareidolia imagery and composing these poems I am asking questions about the world around us, how we perceive and interact with it. This method of constructing a poem is made all the more powerful when the building bricks arrive from seemingly random places and at different times from contributors across the World Wide Web. The coincidences and connections within this exploration of the combined unconscious might indicate to some that a greater influence is at work, or may seem to others to be a glimpse into the secret workings of the creative processes within the poet's mind. There will be some, no doubt, who do not consider these writings as poems at all, yet the list poem in all its variants is a well established form of contemporary creative writing. Furthermore, within each poem there are still traces of the poet's current thoughts and mood, his or her current and childhood experiences, background history, and accumulated knowledge. Surely conveying all these things in words using the poet's own creative vision is how poets approach more conventional work? In his introduction to *Surrealist Poetry in English*, 1978, Edward B. Germain reminds us that in their exploration of the unconscious mind, the Surrealist poets, particularly in England, "*...saw themselves descended from the tradition of the romantics. They looked back with interest to the dream literature of Coleridge's 'Ancient Mariner' and the hallucinatory clarity of 'Kubla Khan'... to the fantasies of Edward Lear and to Lewis Carroll.*" In short, they believed the foundations of their world were laid by literary household names such as these.

I consider that what some may see as a conventional method of experiencing the world around us, and the writing of similes from these observations, as only a small step away from what we are concerned with here in these pages. I am aligning myself with the tradition of the Surrealist poets who I think would have enjoyed both the collision and symbiosis between the individual elements of these poems, as well as the playful process of their creation. I struggle to sum things up better than Mel Gooding, who said of the Surrealists' practice in his editorial of *A Book of Surrealist Games*, that "*Playful procedures and systematic stratagems provided keys to unlock the door to the unconscious and to relate the visual and verbal poetry of collective creativity... Surrealist games and procedures are intended to free the words and images from the constraints of rational and discursive order, substituting chance and indeterminacy for premeditation and deliberation. Surrealism takes the logic and continuity of the dream to have a truly given significance, equalled only by the revelatory power of the unexpected analogy, the marvellous conjunction*". I would like to think there is room for all species of writing on this world, but finally, to those who are still of a mind that the musings of the Surrealist poet are unworthy of a place, I invite you to ponder the words of poet and literary critic, Herbert Read who proposed that "*What [The Surrealist poet] offers to society is not a bagful of his own tricks, his idiosyncrasies, but rather some knowledge of the secrets to which he has had access, the secrets of the self which are buried in every man alike...*"

Some of the methodology here shares similarities with the infamous Rorschach Test or other inkblot psychological tests in which a subject's interpretations of patterns are recorded and then analysed. Therefore, you might well expect the interpretations of a writer to reflect their state of mind whilst composing poems from the patterns in drinks, but any deeper psychological analysis will have to be left to the speculation of the reader.

I hope that you enjoy leafing through my alternative and surreal world, and that next time you pause to enjoy a drink, you might stop and ponder the richer details of our lives. Look through the eyes of the poet within you, even if you may not have found them yet, or if like mine, they require spectacles to see more clearly.

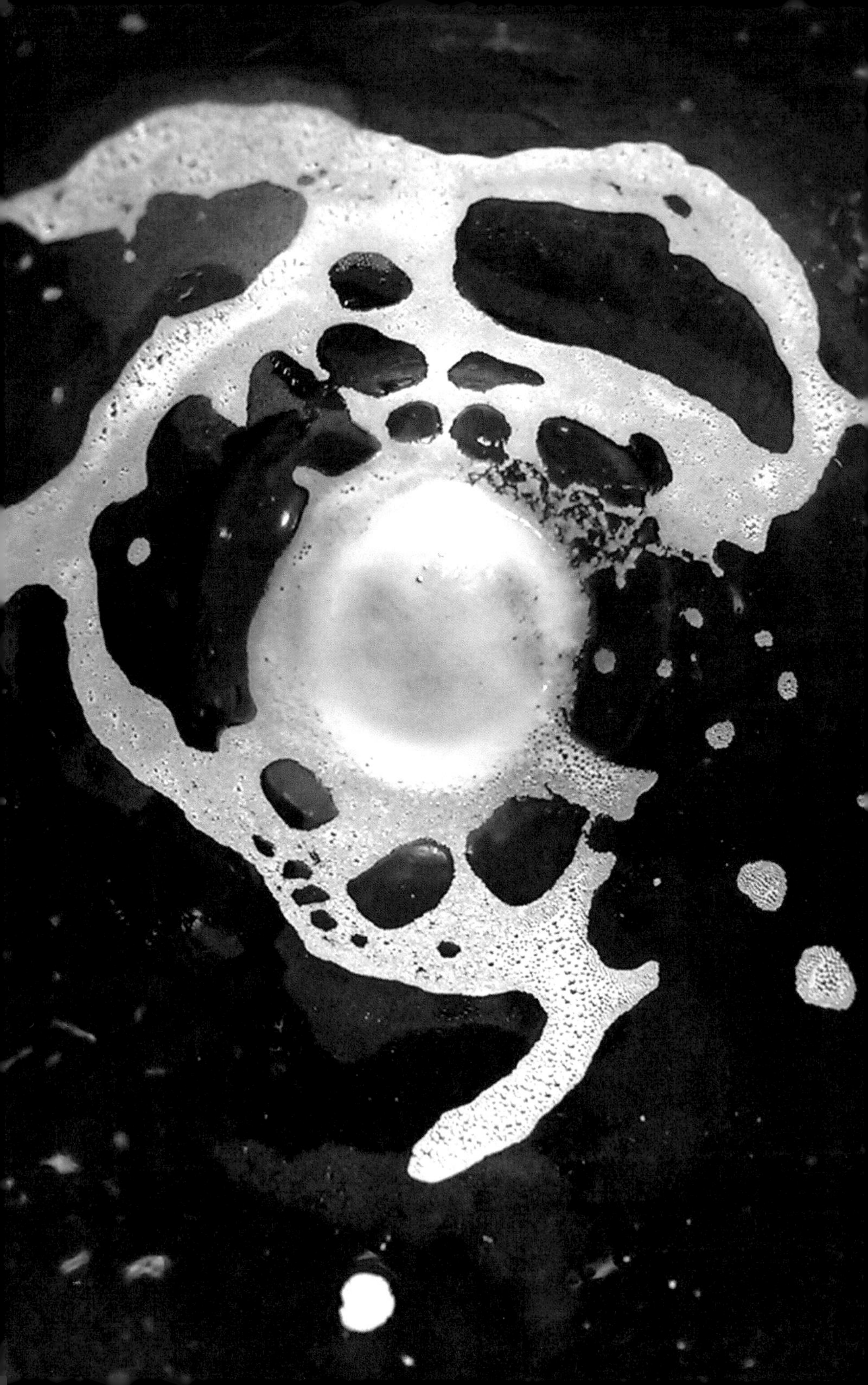

1 Glass Half Full

Belgian Lace

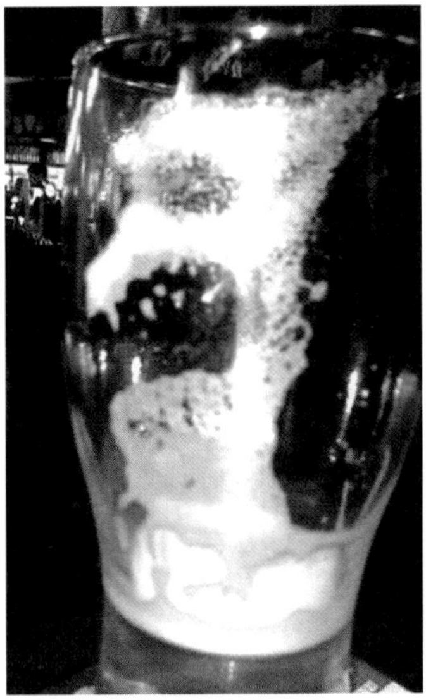

The poems in this opening section have been composed by observing patterns on the surface froth or 'head' of beers and lagers ('*foam*' in the US), and patterns made on the sides of the glass as the beverages are being drunk.

These patterns are sometimes referred to as lacing, or rather more exotically, *Belgian* or *Brussels Lace,* and are seen by some as an indicator or the beer's quality. They are influenced by factors such as how fast the drink is quaffed, alcohol content, and even how the glass has been cleaned, but here of course we are concerned more with the artistic interpretation of their form.

Some of the poems (where indicated) are composed from comments gathered via Facebook. In these cases, contributors are listed in the same order that their lines appear in the poem. Otherwise all words and images are the work of the author.

Above: 'The Glass Dragon' courtesy of Robin Parker

Two Cats Kissing

Bengali

Ayres Rock, *sip* [1]
Willy Wisp, *sip* [2]
A crudely drawn horse, *sip*
Two cats kissing, *sip*
Cows' udders, *sip*
A thistle head, *sip*
A deep-sea diver's helmet, *sip*
Empty

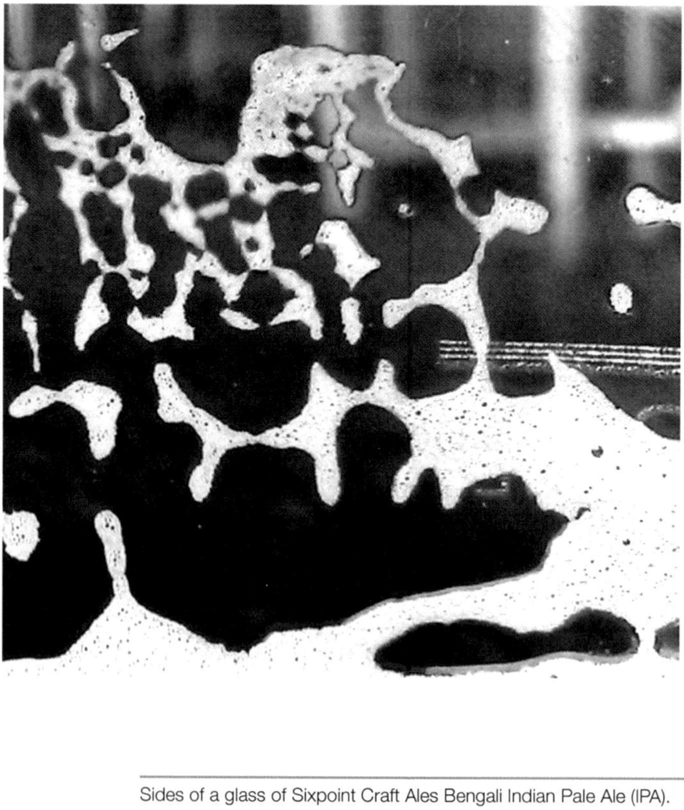

Sides of a glass of Sixpoint Craft Ales Bengali Indian Pale Ale (IPA).
Table 28, The Percy Shaw, Halifax.

Stone Skipping
Honey Porter

Batman, *sip* [3]
Heart locket, *sip*
An indoor boomerang, *sip* [4]
An anteater wearing a trilby, *sip*
Someone fly-fishing, *sip*
A kiwi, *sip* [5]
A stone skipping on water, *sip* [6]
Profile of a lion, *sip*
An emu looking backwards, *sip*
Sustrans waymarker, *sip* [7]
Oakley sports sunglasses, *sip* [8]
A Kateroo, *empty* [9]

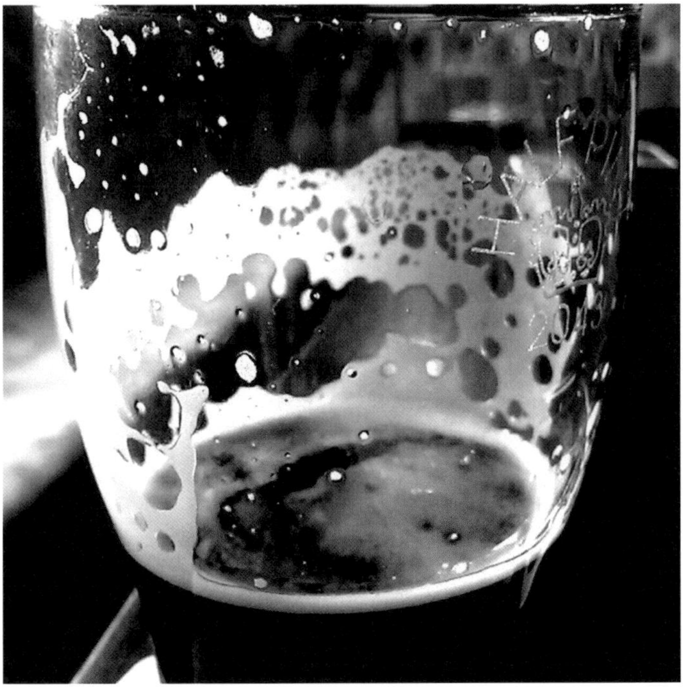

Sides of a half-pint glass of honey porter after each sip.
The Golden Lion, Todmorden.

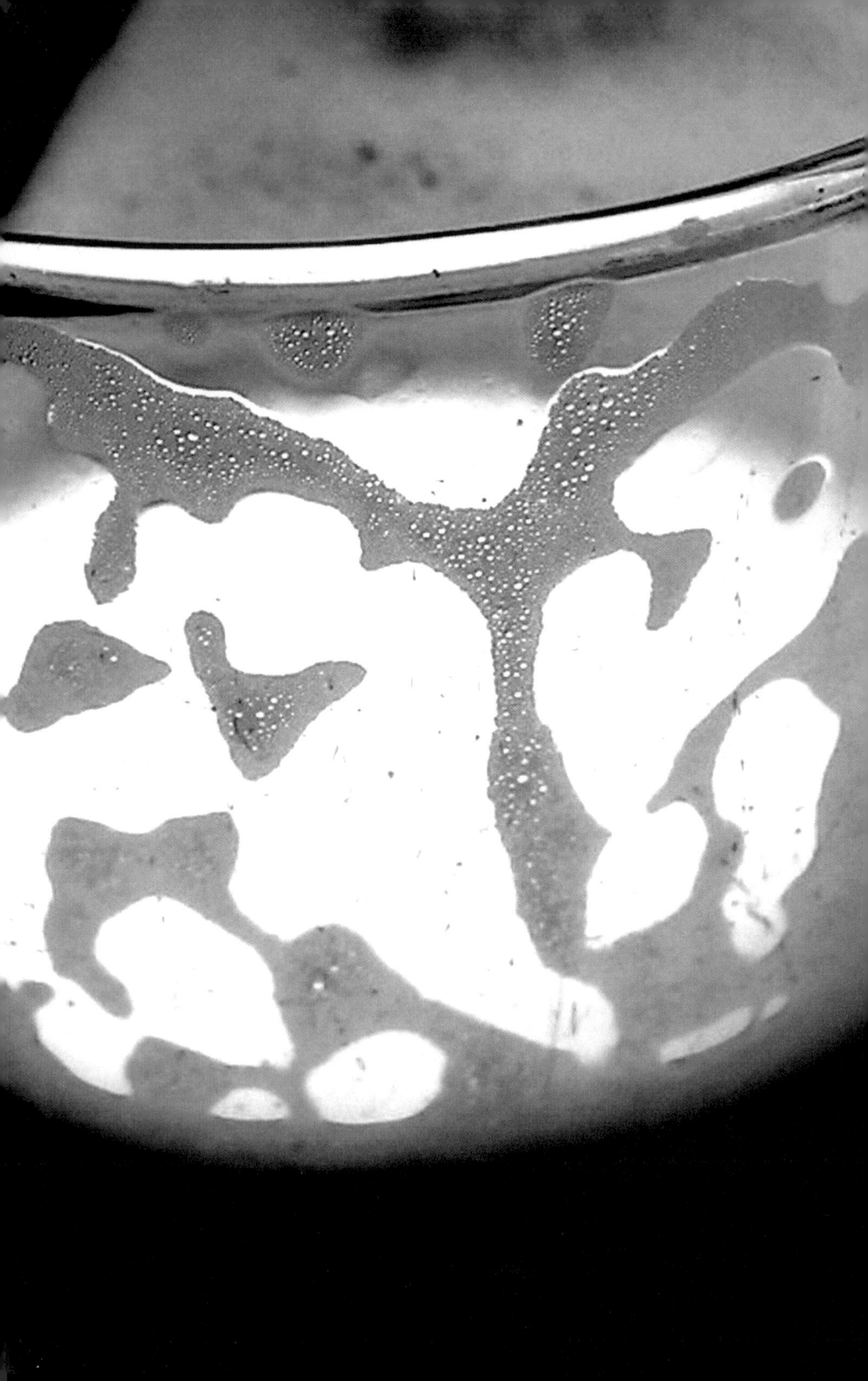

Playing Football in the Style of Matisse
Blonde Witch

A painting by Matisse [10]

Wrestlers on the left and a Playboy Bunny
(somewhat deformed) on the right

The ghost of Pac-Man [11]

Punch & Judy [12]

Flux capacitor [13]

Figure featured in the film poster for 300 [14]

A baby elephant drinking from a stream under rocks

Inspector Clouseau [15]

Fish and sad octopus

A punk with a hooked nose about to punch a pumpkin
with already serious facial injuries

A slightly sinister pumpkin face with a hat on!

Men playing football in the style of Matisse

A pelvis

Al Catpone [16]

Zig and Zag and a cat with missing jigsaw pieces [17]

An elephant bowing before a horrified fish

A big scared ghost being chased by a little scared ghost

A member of the band, Ceiling Demons [18]

Freddy Krueger [19]

Mr Punch and a spooky ghost.

Sides of a half-pint glass of Moorhouses Blonde Witch.
The Shears (aka The Paris Gates), Halifax.

Contributors: *Gaia Holmes, Andrew Marsh, Maisy Howell, John Lusardi, Skye Darkwoods, Dave Barnes, Sara Robinson, Valerie Anderson Gaskill, Daniel Galef, Rachel McGladdery, Rosie Blunn, Rachel Bond, Christina Rothenbeck, Marion Oxley, Wayneo Martyn Stankiewicz, Clare Johnston, Louise Fazackerley, William Thirsk-Gaskill, Valerie Anderson Gaskill and Clare Wakefield.*

Top to Bottom

Ritual

Nothing, sip
Buttocks or breasts, *sip*
Nothing, sip
Nothing, sip
Nothing, sip
Nothing, sip
Nothing, sip
Nothing, sip
Nothing, sip
A mouth of sharp teeth, *sip*

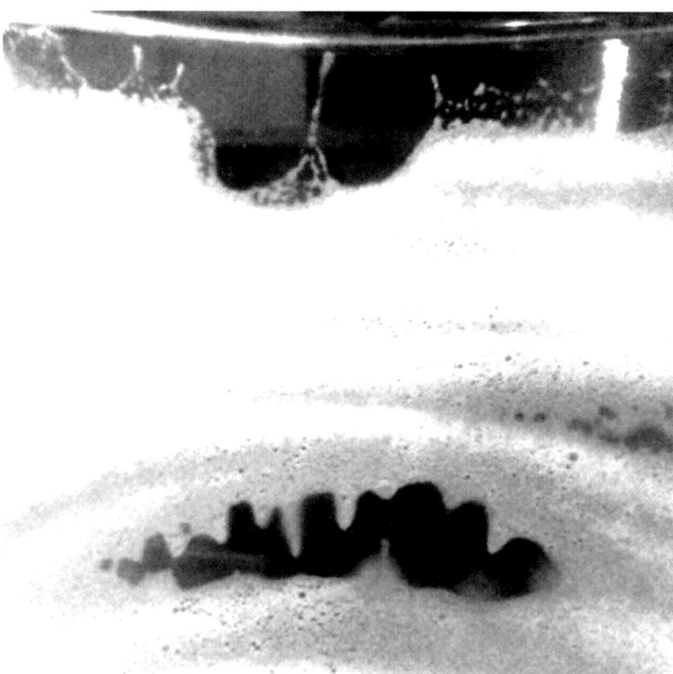

Sides of a half-pint glass of Alchemy Brewery, Ritual IPA.
The Stockbridge Tap, Edinburgh.

Telephone Chess
Pentland

Two people playing chess across a table, *sip*
A giraffe and fox standoff, *sip*
An old-fashioned telephone, *sip*
Bee monsters from an old episode of Dr Who [20]
A kiwi, *sip*
Nothing, sip
Seahorse's head, *sip*
Nothing, sip
Upper case letter 'M', *sip*
Nothing, sip
Elongated Superlambanana, *sip* [21]
Empty.

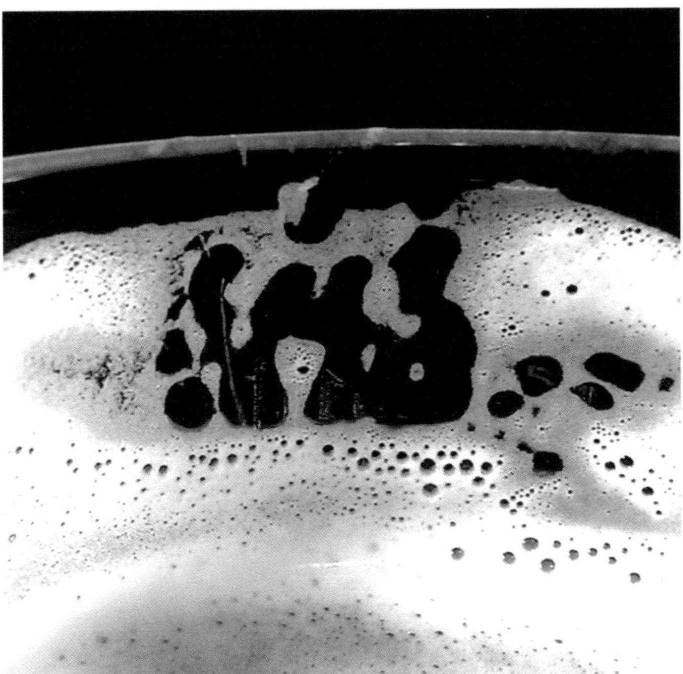

Surface and sides of a half-pint glass of Stewart Brewing, Pentland IPA. The Flotterstone Inn, near Penicuik.

Piano Curling
Caledonian Deuchars

A figure delivering a curling stone [22]
Piano soloist in a tailcoat
prepares to press play on ghetto blaster. [23]

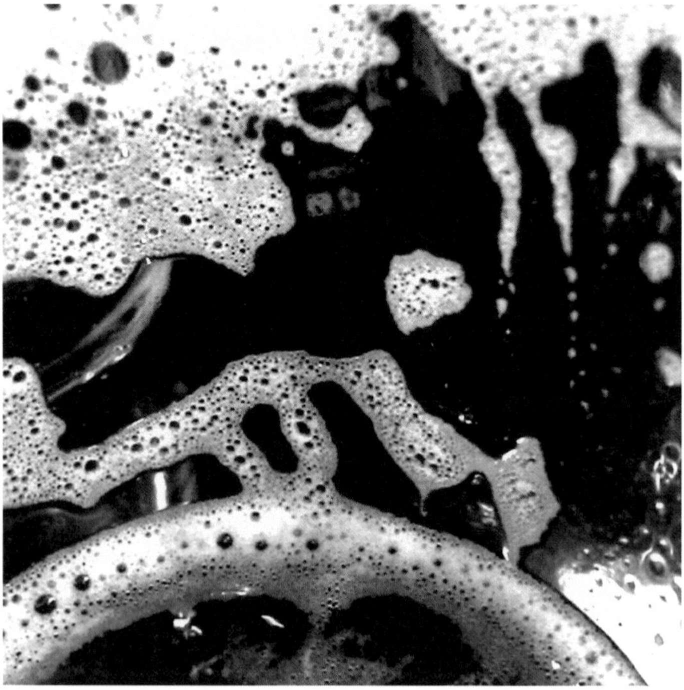

Sides of a half-pint glass of Caledonian Brewing Company's Deuchars IPA.Table 32, The Percy Shaw, Halifax.

Composed *by: the author and David Ford.*
Above graphic: Sochi 2014 Curling Symbol.

Shark Fins
Black Bee Porter

Cashmere, *sip* [24]
A Henry Moore style reclining figure, *sip* [25]
A boot, *sip*
Snowflakes falling and settling, *sip*
A figure heading a football, *sip*
A shark fin, *sip*
Solar flares, *sip* [26]
The shark fin travelling in the opposite direction, *sip*
The face of The Traveler, *sip* [27]
Empty

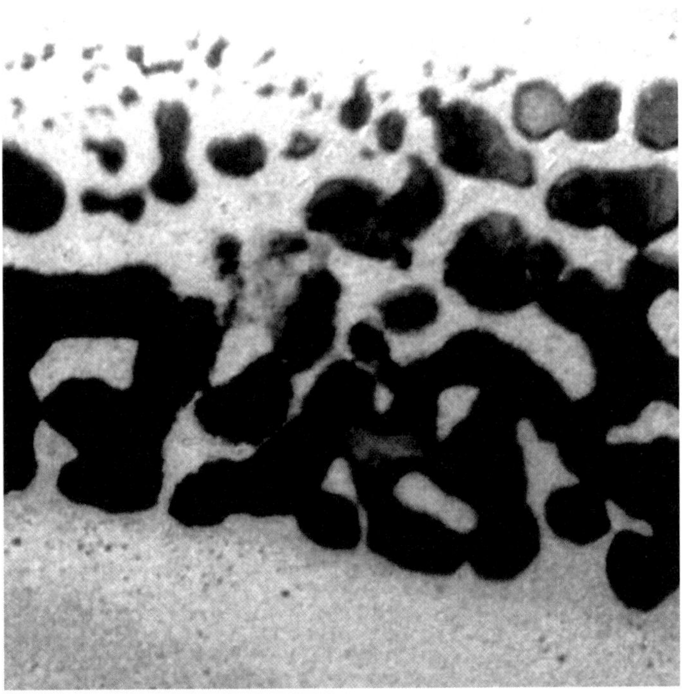

Surface and sides of a half pint of Phoenix Black Bee Porter after each sip. The Three Pigeons, Halifax.

The Surprise Reappearance of New Zealand

Corona Extra

New Zealand, *pour*
A vertical duck silhouette, *pour*
Chakra diagram, *pour* [28]
Trailing seaweed, *pour*
New Zealand (again), *pour*
Man wearing beret, *pour*, *swirl* [29]
Three headed electric rotary razor, *pour*
Flower with five petals, *pour*, *swirl*
A lung, *pour*
Mud geyser erupting, *swirl*
Nothing.

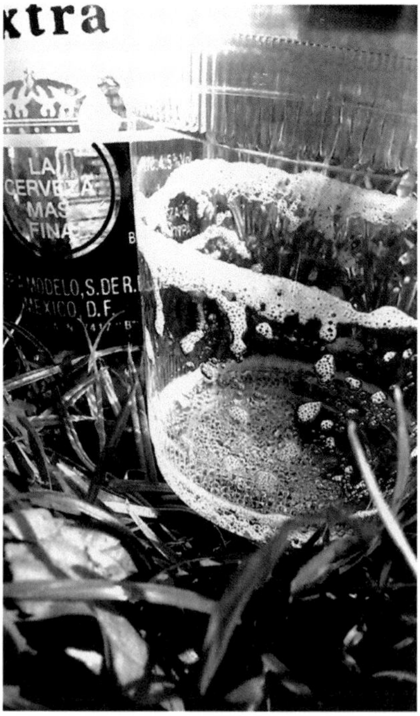

From the surface of a disposable white plastic cup and reflections in a bottle of Corona Extra Lager. Orchard (Brae) Park, Edinburgh.

Distant Rain Dance [30]

The Bore

Distant hills with residual snow, *sip*

Barbed wire, *sip*

Profile of a plump face, *sip*

A crude henge, *sip* [30]

Someone with tribal hair
dancing under a cloud, *sip*

Empty.

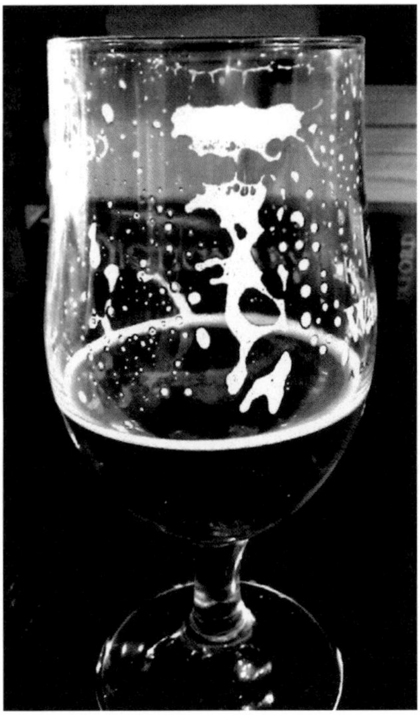

Sides of a half-pint glass of The Bore Pale Ale.
The Albion Hotel, Arnside.

Jointly *composed with Gaia Holmes*

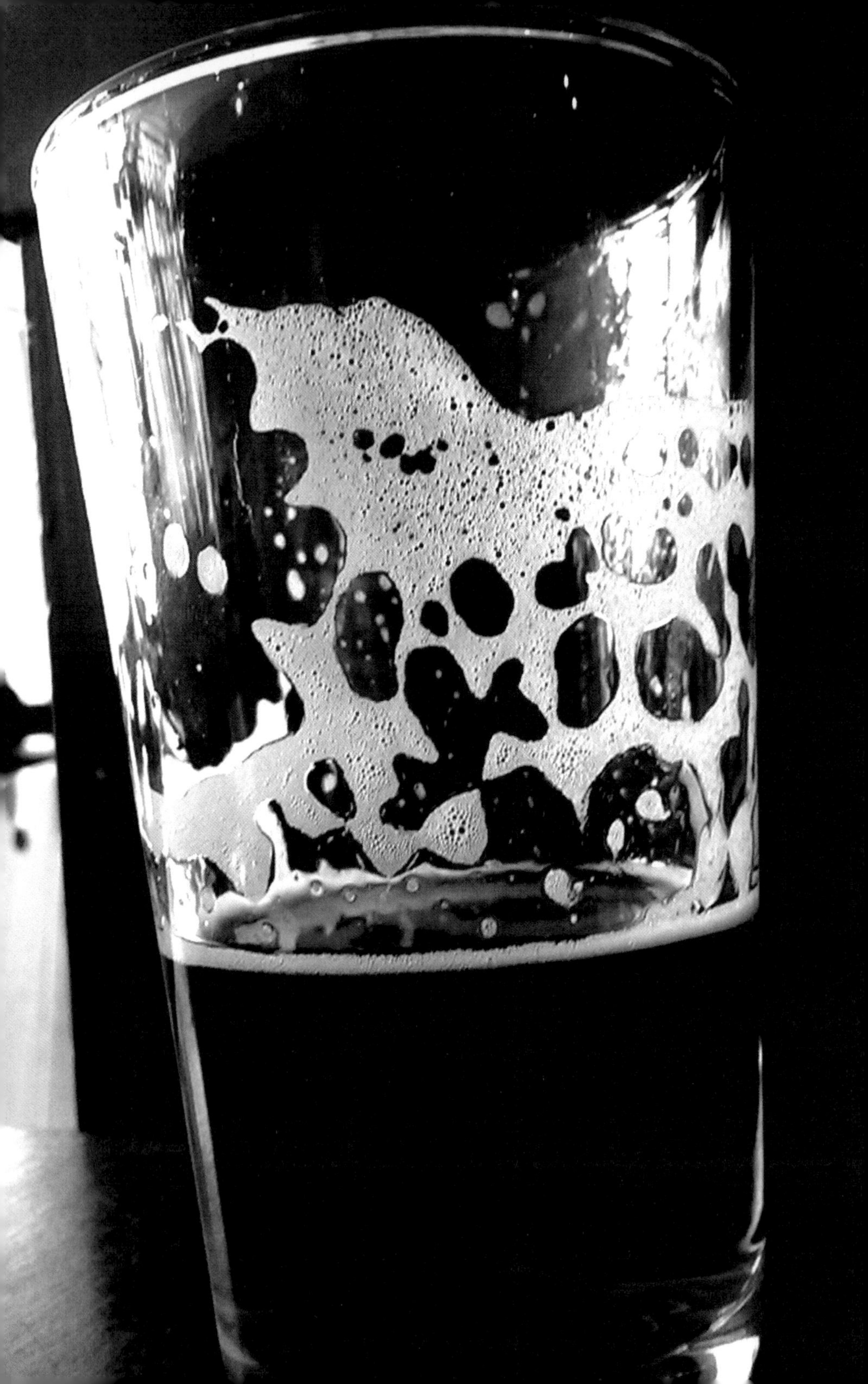

May I Have the Next Dance

Saltaire Cascade

A lizard shrugging his shoulders

The Bonsai Great Cthulhu erupting out of the
peaty depths of the ocean from behind the stars [31]

A unicorn... No wait... a slug [32]

The words 'P_od kbo'

Horse

A Scooby-Doo ghost! [33]

Mickey Mouse laughing at a beached whale [34]

Elvis at the end of the night, quiff wilting

Cretan bull leaping [35]

Elvis (reprise) [36]

Mr Blobby [37]

A whale leaping out of the sea

Fish, rocks and a jellyfish

Jellyfish on a beach

Screaming ghosts

Hokey pokey

Bat-Cat

A winged beast

Snoopy caught in a rock avalanche
with suspect dragon fleeing [38]

Ecce homo [39]

Dancing ghosts

A giant slug crawling over a koala

A juggling flamenco dancer [40]

Half the logo of the Llanelli Scarlets Rugby Union team.

Sides of a half-pint glass of Saltaire Brewery Cascade IPA.
The Old Gate, Hebden Bridge.

Contributors: *Tony Halsall, Colin Robinson, Drew Marsh, Tony Burger, Julie Rose-Clark, Rachel McGladdery, Cathy Bryant, Sarah L. Dixon, Steven Waling, Rachel McGladdery, Steve Fiddle, Gaia Holmes, Gillie Carpenter, Liz Wells, Sebastian Degorce, Peppy Hills, David Jarman, Keiron Higgins, Marion Oxley, John Lusardi, Catherine Gaboreau, Winston Plowes, Rosie Blunn and Tudor Gwynn.*

Tanks on the White House Lawn

Bengali

Paw Print
Mould
Hot chocolate
A telephone
The Gobi Desert [41]
A monkey face
Gypsy tart from 70's school dinners [42]
A telephone
Tanks on The White House lawn [43]
The Cow jumping over the moon [44]
A telephone
Paw print.

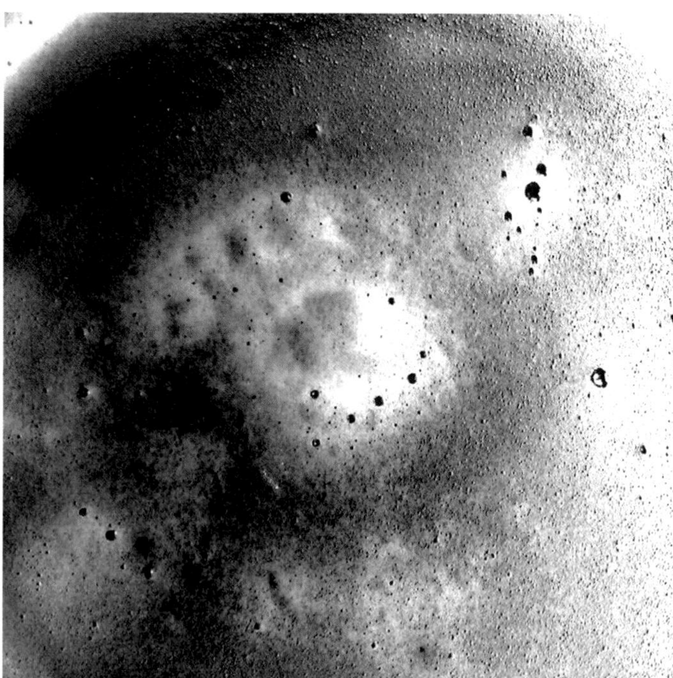

Surface of a glass of Sixpoint Craft Ales Bengali IPA.
Table 28, The Percy Shaw, Halifax.

Contributors: *Genevieve L. Walsh, Steve Fiddle, Sarah L. Dixon, Liz Wells, Bob Horne, David Clegg, Valerie Anderson Gaskill, Jax Westmoreland, Freddie Philips, Julie Rose-Clark, Gaia Holmes and Maisy Howell.*

The Scream

Bengali

The Scream [45]

A foetus

Milky coffee

A marshmallow

Craters

Screaming woman with an open mouth,
wide eyes and a shock of dark hair

Penguin under a bough of snow

A creamy marshmallow man

The Scream.

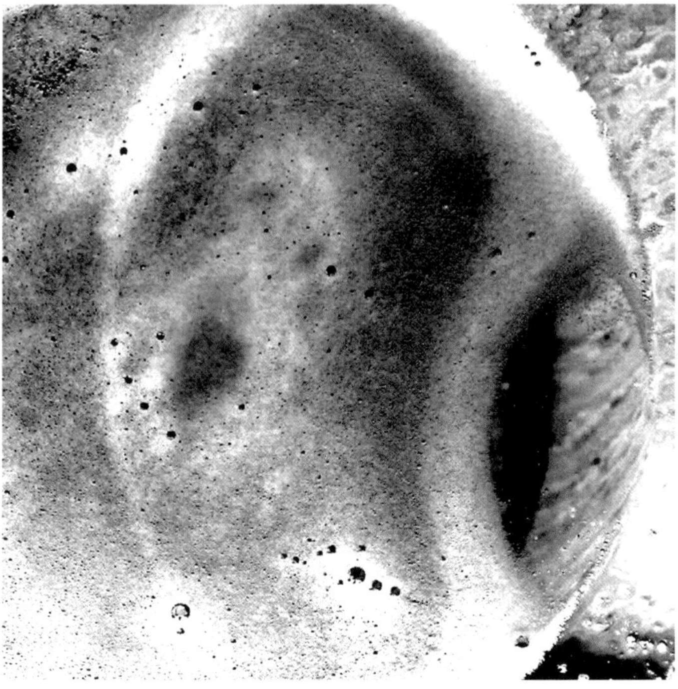

Surface of a glass of Sixpoint Craft Ales Bengali IPA.
Table 28, The Percy Shaw, Halifax.

Contributors: *Catherine Heartfield, Genevieve L. Walsh, Steve Fiddle, Sarah L. Dixon, Steve Fiddle (second contribution), David Clegg, Valerie Anderson Gaskill, Steven Waling and Jax Westmoreland.*

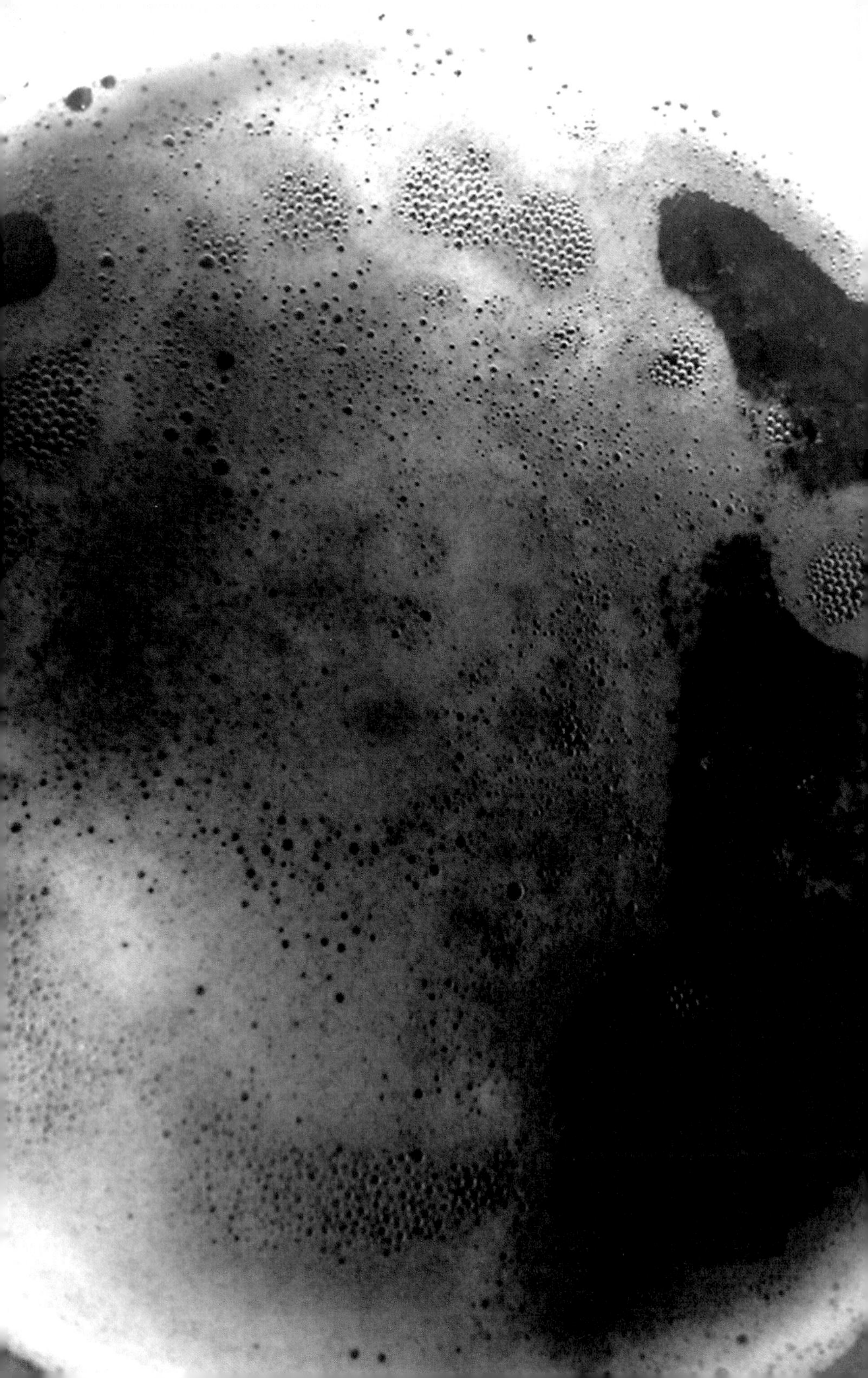

The Perforated Edge of Heaven

Homebrew

Pour, Cross-section through a Crunchie Bar [46]
Links of a chain breaking
Two hearts coalescing
An anvil, *sip*
A chick, *sip*
Lips slowly closing, *sip*
A paper bag being twisted by its corners, *sip*
Someone singing hymns with hands
offered up to heaven, *sip*
The perforated edge of a page torn
from a spiral-bound notebook, *sip*
Empty.

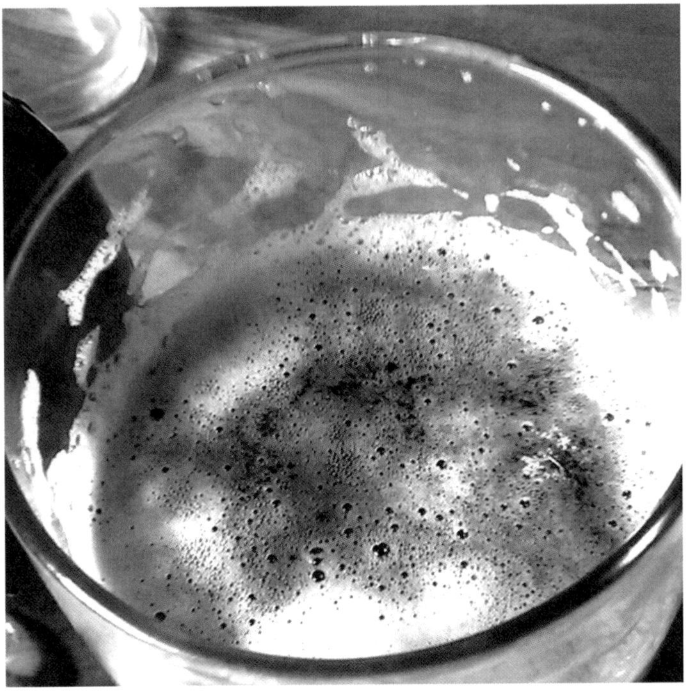

Sides and surface of a pint glass of Steve Senior's Homebrew stout. Narrowboat on The Rochdale Canal.

Bicycle Handlebars
Orkney Stout

Antlers, *sip*
A bicycle, *sip*
A handlebar moustache, *sip* [47]
Hand shadow of an evil face, *sip*
A goblin, *sip*
A kiwi, *sip*
Springboard diver in a tuck, *sip*
Bearskin rug, *sip*
Spider monkey, *sip* [48]
Empty.

Sides of a half-pint glass of Highland Brewing Co (Swannay Brewery) Stout after each sip.
The Stockbridge Tap, Edinburgh.

Goat Wattles

Cascade

Goat Wattles, *sip* [49]
A vertical strip light, *sip*
The shoulders of Whernside, *sip* [50]
Nothing, sip
Waking vision of a window, *sip*
Angry tribal face, *sip*
A screenshot from the puzzle App Brain Dots, *sip* [51]
Berk from The Trapdoor, *sip* [52]
Wind cherub, *sip* [53]
Face of a conga eel, *sip* [54]
Empty
Rabbit / jester.

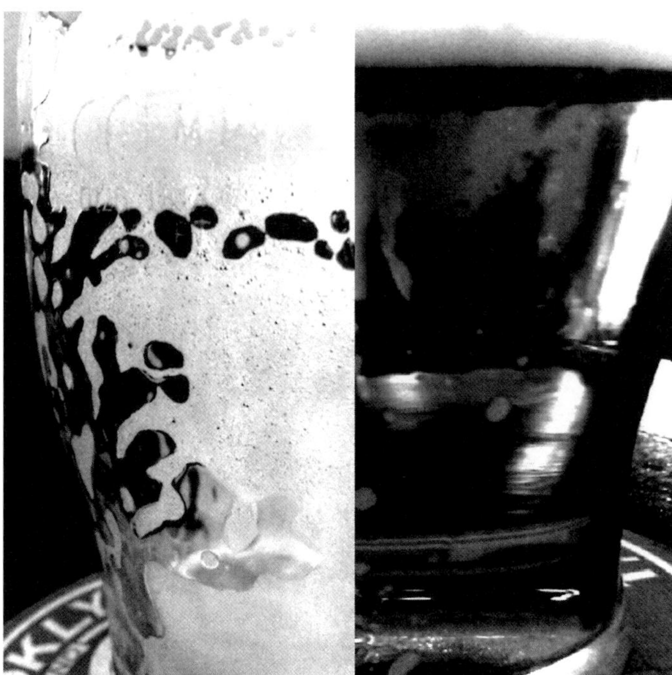

Reflections within and patterns on the inside and outside of a half-pint glass of Saltaire Brewery Cascade Pale Ale.
The Old Gate, Hebden Bridge.

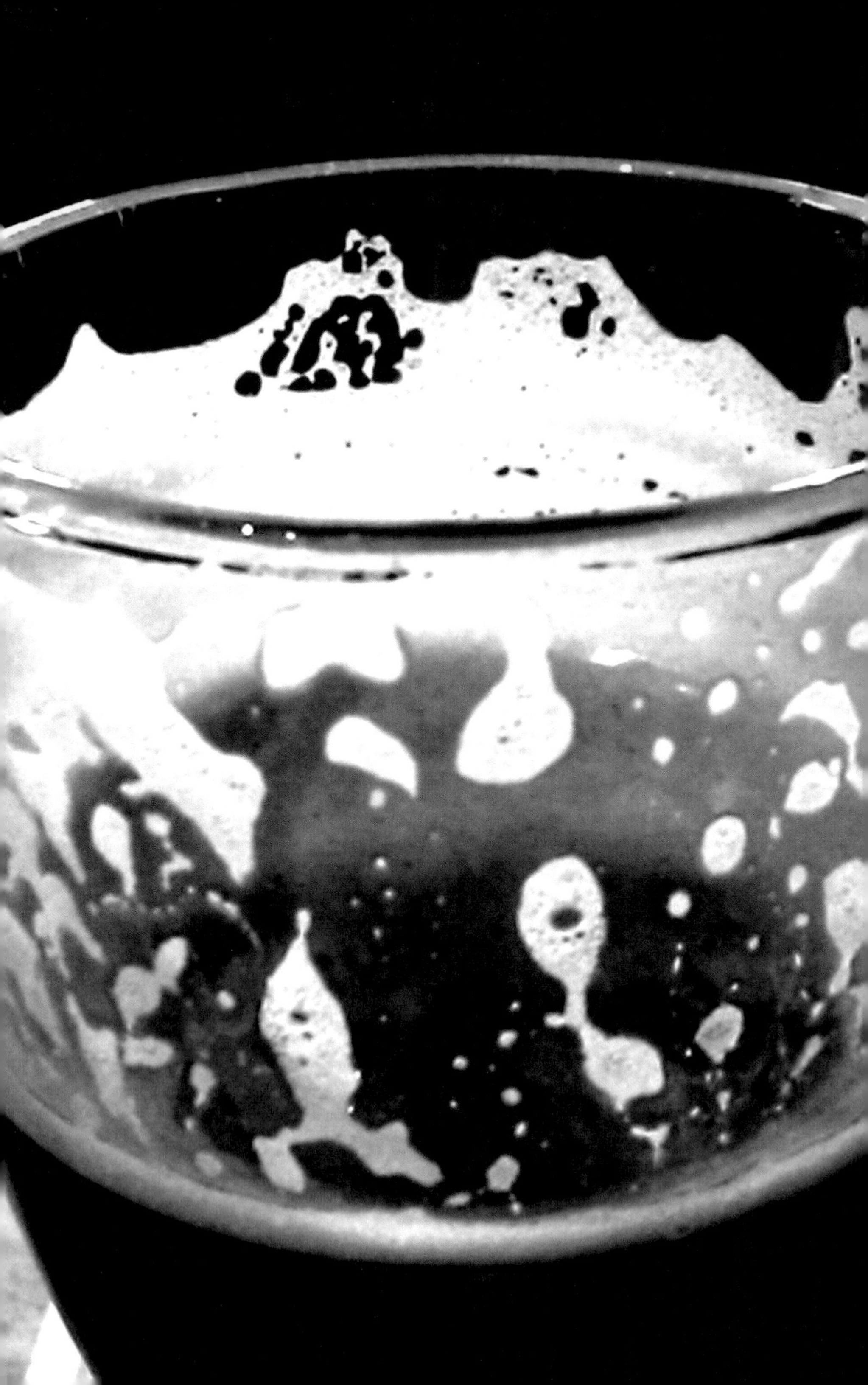

Tintin et la Fusée Italienne [55]

Stoodley Stout

A snow capped mountain with cave people
People running
Outer space with a little rocket!
Surprised Pinocchio [56]
Amoebas splitting in half to make two identical new amoebas [57]
A Joan Miró (foreground) [58]
Ansel Adams (background) [59]
The rocket and Italy!
Rocket ship.
A wolf and a dog
The Eternal Wave (back)
Blobby aliens and a rocket (front)
The rocket, a cockroach with a balloon, and Italy
Nora Batty [60]
Will-o'-the-wisps, and ghosts [61]
A sly fox (right), and a little rocket (middle)
Alien, rocket and ghost all moving in a sea of ale
Tintin's rocket!

Sides of a half-pint glass of Little Valley Brewery Stoodley Stout. The Works, Sowerby Bridge.

Contributors: *Su Senior, Andy Smith, Deborah Cunliffe, Connor MacLeod, Tudor Gwynn Steven Waling, Gillie Carpenter, Joe Williams, Justine Knight, Rachel McGladdery, Cathy Bryant, Matthew Nicholson, John Lusardi, Elly O'Grady, Catherine Gaboreau and Caroline Sturges.*

Jellyfish in Triplicate

Bengali

Jellyfish
Love heart
Conjoined twins having a staring competition [62]
The moon
Jellyfish
Water going down a plughole
Volcano ready to erupt
The mark on wet sand above a cockle
Jellyfish.

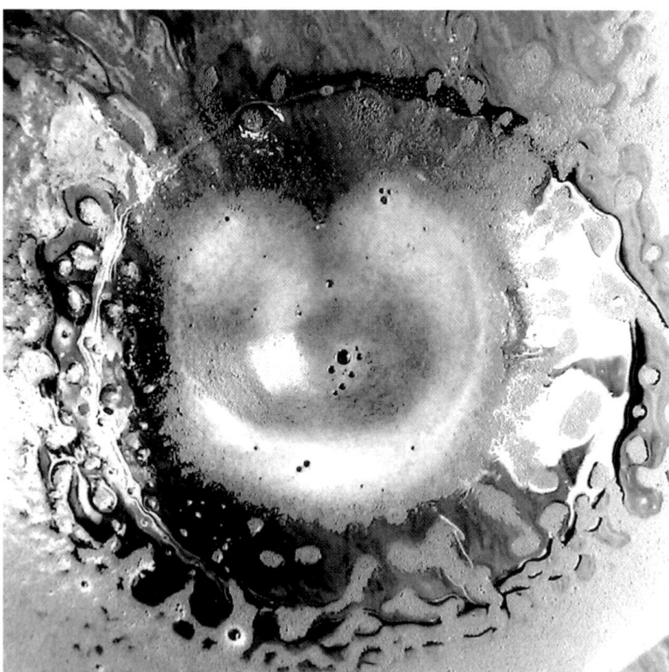

Surface of a glass of Sixpoint Craft Ales Bengali IPA.
Table 28,The Percy Shaw, Halifax.

Contributors: *Ric Taylor, Genevieve L. Walsh, Catherine Heartfield, Sarah L. Dixon, Nicky Vaux, Bob Horne, Liz Wells, Rachel McGladdery and Mark Connors.*

Twitcher [63]

Homebrew

A sandpiper racing left [64]
A hunkered-down Western gull
An elephant
Oystercatcher [65]
Bubble bird.

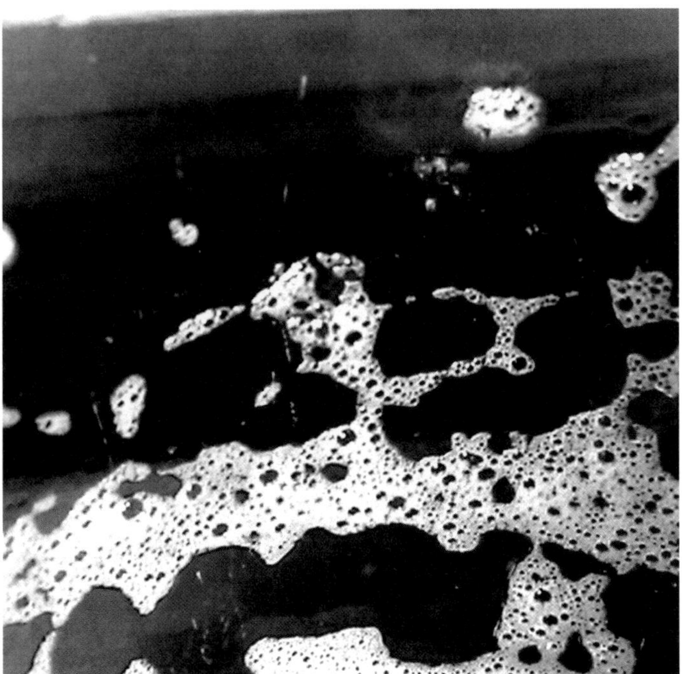

Sides of a pint glass of Steve Senior's Homebrew.
Narrowboat on The Rochdale Canal, Hebden Bridge.

Contributors: *Winston Plowes, Sheila Sondik, Maisy Howell, Jos Murphy and Ben Cornish.*

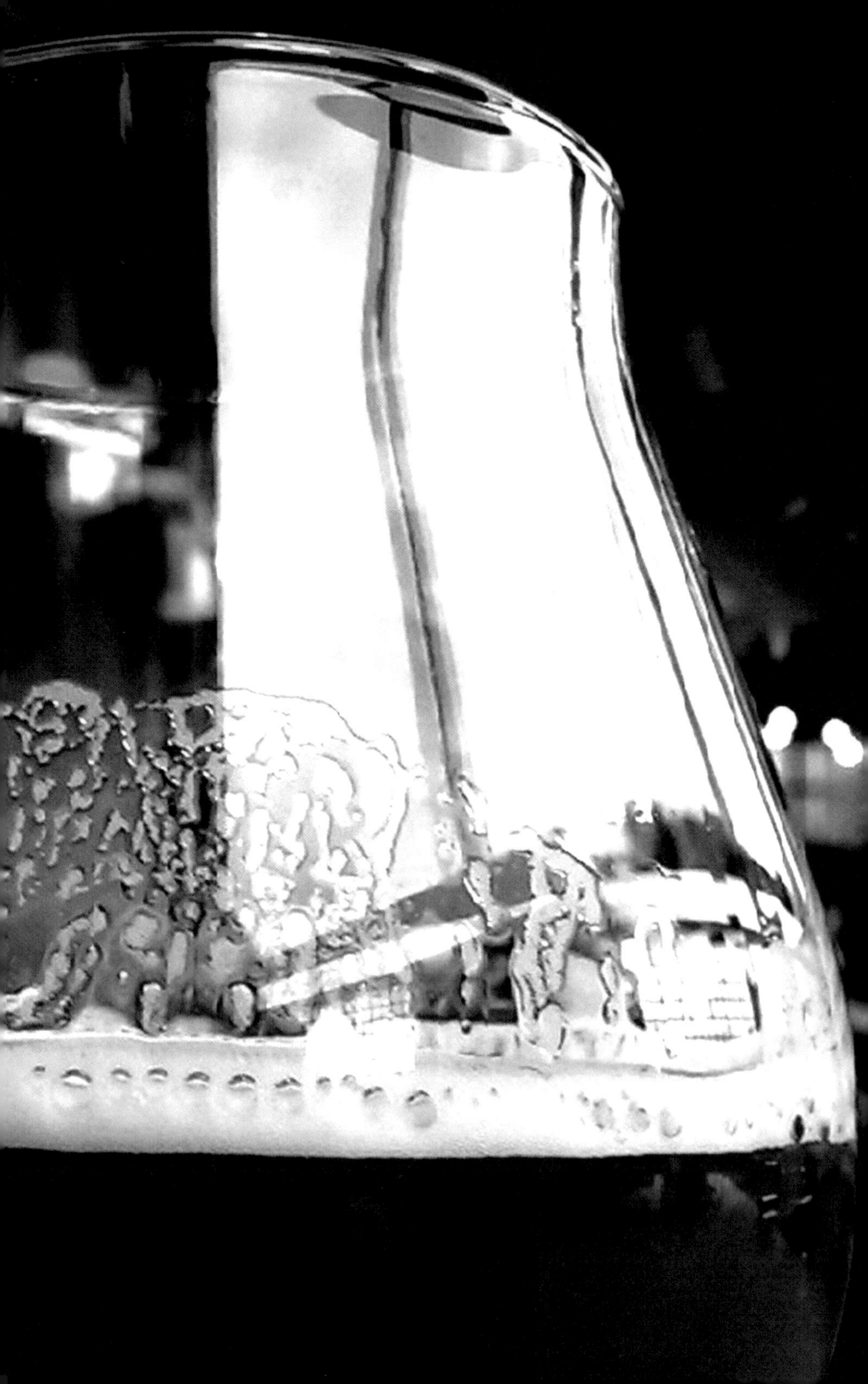

Girl With the Wind in Her Hair

Premier

FULL
sip
A Jellyfish
sip
A Hammerhead shark
sip
A girl with the wind in her hair
sip
Pac-Man
sip
A Serpent / Dragon
sip
A magpie
sip
A bucking horse
sip
A high heel boot
sip
EMPTY.

Sides of a pint glass of Moorhouses Premier Bitter after each sip.
The Trades Club, Hebden Bridge.

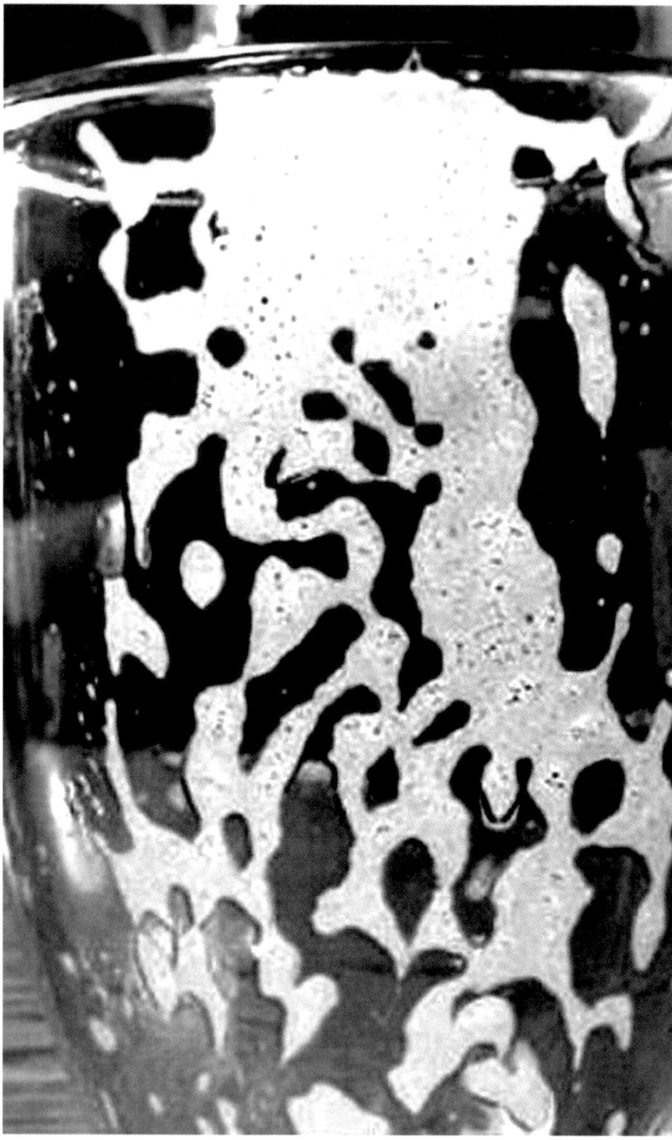

Sides of a pint glass of Alchemy Brewery, Ritual IPA.
The Stockbridge Tap, Edinburgh.

Contributors: *Maisy Howell, Keiron Higgins, Andrew Lawson, Kath Thorpe, William Thirsk-Gaskill, Dave Barnes, Cathy Bryant (2 lines), Aylin Erengül Gregg, Jax Westmoreland, Rose Drew, Winston Plowes, Connor MacLeod, Steven Waling, Linda Hodges, Julie Rose-Clark, Charlie Carr, Rachel McGladdery, Mark Connors, Mab Jones, Lazlo Palko, David Jarman, John Lusardi, Rosie Blunn, Geneviève L. Walsh, Tudor Gwynn, Katherine Coussement, Sébastien Jean Degorce, Bob Horne, Marion Oxley and Cat Kinson.*

Pandas Versus Cows

Ritual

Panda

The Elephant Man with two faces [66]

Angry Panda

A grimacing Ewok [67]

A Bull

A basketball player slam-dunking
into a leaping dolphin's mouth

Cthulhu [31]

A mermaid dancing
while a man plays the piano to her left

A cow

Alligator eating people

Dr Who opening titles

A bull

Mantis shrimp

SpongeBob SquarePants in the pulpit [68]

Little baby ghostlets

Circus Performers

A Zebra's head

Monty Burns/Bart Simpson chimera [69]

A Dalmatian dog from behind

Octo-goat

Dead people

Ghostly Bart Simpson

Pirates treasure map

Carnival

Either the Elephant Man or Morrissey
wearing wearing a massive joke shop false nose

A player in a New Orleans jazz funeral band

Flamenco dancer [40]

Cthulhu

The West Coast of Scotland

Matisse off cuts

A heartless dancing man balancing on the fingertips
of his right hand and part of his head

The heel, foot and calf of an unidentified person

The laying of an egg falling past a gloved hand

Cow.

Sides of a pint glass of Bad Co Brewery, Wild Gravity IPA.
The Big Six, Halifax.

Contributors: *Tudor Gwynn, Skye Darkwoods, Keiron Higgins, Andrew Marsh, Joanna Crosby, Petrova C Fairhurst, Dave Barnes, Joe Williams, Rose Condo, Rachel McGladdery, Valerie Chapman, Geneviève L. Walsh, Laura Rzhepishevska, David Jarman, Cathy Bryant, Jennifer Gaye Gardner, Cathy Bryant (2 lines), Carol Robson, Sarah Jackson, Kim Lana Blackburn, Andrew Lawson, Michaela O'Sullivan, George McKim, Brian Toberman, Clare Johnston, Ben Cornish, Dave Jellybean, Nik Robot-King, Diana Forrest, Maisy Howell, Terry Woodward, David Ford, Martin Long, Mark Brosc Broscombe and Marion Oxley.*

The Mercator Projection of Endor [70, 71]

Wild Gravity

A running horse speeding through night mist
Stormtrooper helmet [72]
A crocodile with an overly large nose
A lamb
A flock of black-faced sheep
A frog
The world map from 1960-70s BBC ident [73]
Africa and South America, in the wrong places
A Wookiee and a Stormtrooper snogging [74, 72]
A wide faced skellybob [75]
A herd of black-faced sheep
Scooby-Doo ghost
A big family of dogs coming to the beach
Bison battering through a landlslide
Two skulls taking a drunken selfie
Black lambs in a bubble bath
The Loch Ness Monster, swimming amongst curds [76]
Loch Ness monster biting Scooby-Doo
Black faced sheep
Crocodile
Bubble dragon entering from the right, breathing soapy fire
Two rutting stag beetles! [77]
Stormtrooper helmet from Star Wars
Dogs sniffing each other's bums
Little dog with its ears cocked, looking at its reflection in a puddle
Clouds
Bull's head
Zombie Stormtrooper!
Map of an alien planet (Mercator's projection)
Cows
Car wash
Sheep dog
Star Wars Stormtrooper
Scooby-Doo type ghost
A smiling Staffordshire bull terrier tongue hanging out,
running back from the sea.

A Bask of Crocodiles

Bengali

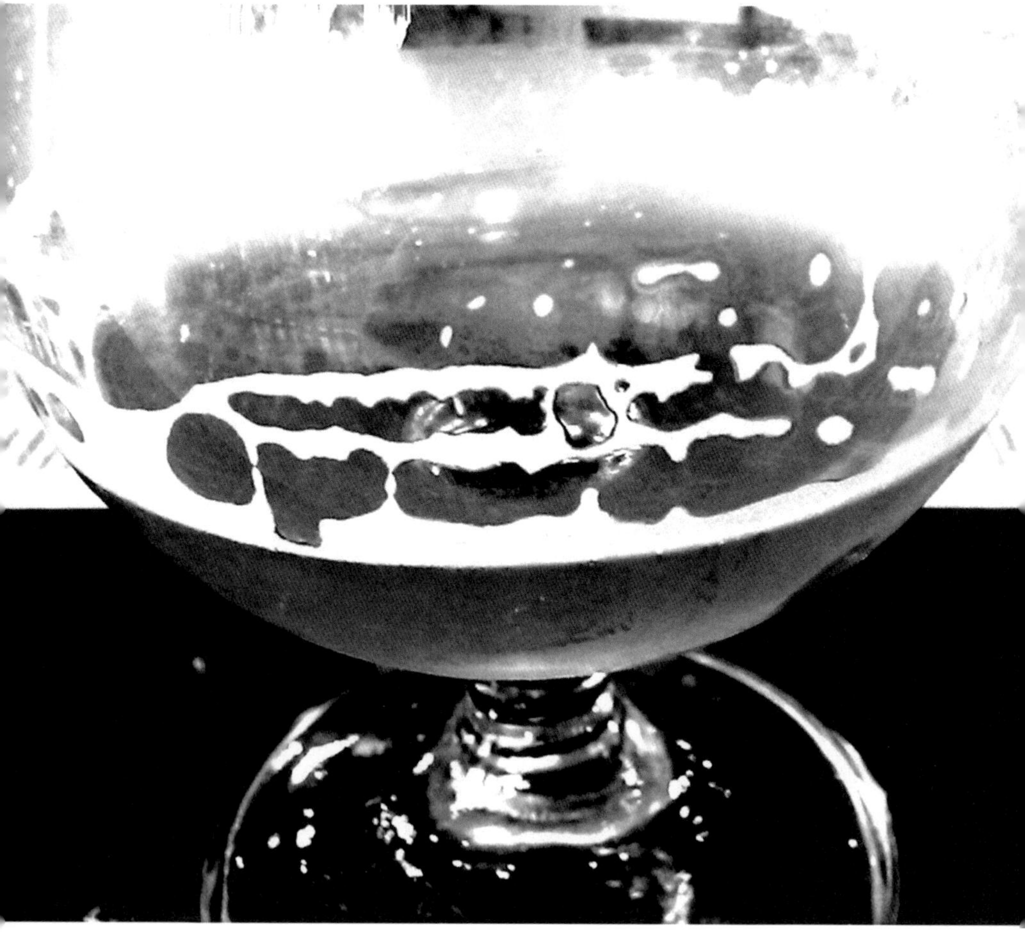

Crocodile

Nutcrackers

A dog chasing a duck

Crocodile/Alligator

Cross channel swimmer

Crumbling stone wall

A dragon enjoying the snow

Sunlight

A fox about to catch a small dragon as it gets eaten

Basking crocodile vs. curious fox

Crocodile with the word 'Opera' beneath it

Head of an Egyptian cat

Crocodile about to eat a puppy

A person i.e. a head with a big hand
trying to catch a flying caterpillar

A gigantic pike
attempting to swallow the island of Honshu [78]

A wolf chasing a duck

Hungry caterpillar!

Roobarb (of Roobarb and Custard)
leaping to the right to catch a duck [79]

A flying alligator about to swallow
a baby Loch Ness monster

Crocodile

Nutcrackers.

Surface of a glass of Sixpoint Craft Ales Bengali IPA.
The Percy Shaw, Halifax.

Contributors: *Winston Plowes, Joe Williams, Tony Burger, Deborah Cunliffe, Joanna Crosby, Robin Turner, Steve Nash, Little Bird, Rachel McGladdery, Rachel Geldard, Wayneo Martyn Stankiewicz, Gillie Carpenter, Julie Rose Clark, Julia Gray, William Thirsk-Gaskill, Diana Forrest, Helen Fitt, Tudor Gwynn, Caroline Sturges and Max Ferrari.*

Oviposium

Stella

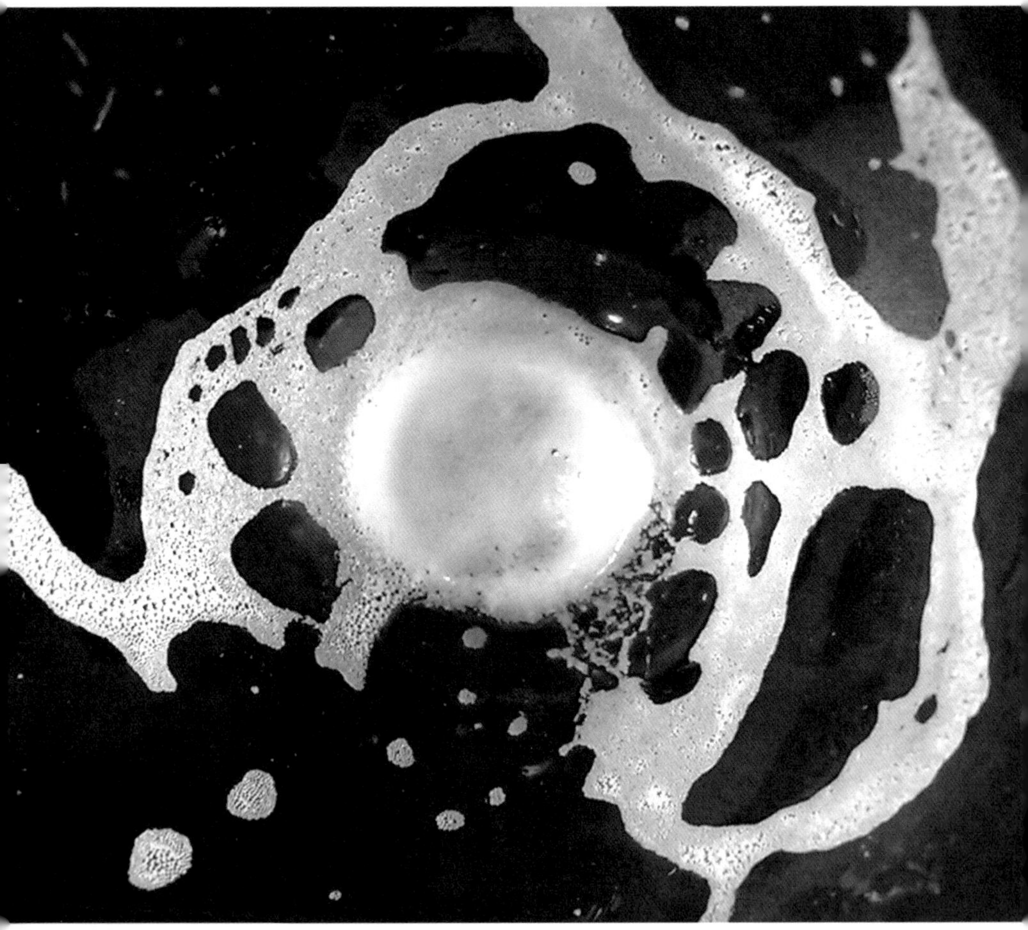

Pig

Fried egg in monochrome

A nipple in the sea

A jellyfish being attacked by a shark

A fish swimming straight at you

Fried egg

A sporty steering wheel

Fried egg

Stag beetle and ibex [77, 80]

An atomic bomb explosion from space

Fried egg

Egg!

Hiroshima at the moment of detonation,
from 10 miles high! [81]

Bernard Manning with yolk on his face
but a very prominent sideburn! [82]

Skeleton fried egg

Slimer from Ghostbusters
being washed down the drain [83]

Egg

Crab with brain slug

Space pig

A hare, a shoal of fish and a whale
jumping over the moon.

Startled one-eyed alien

Underwater emergency button

Sea nipple definitely!

Knuckle-duster for Alex Brooker [84]

Peppa Pig. [85]

Bottom of a half-pint glass of Stella Artois.
The Chinese Buffet, Halifax.

Contributors: *Steve Ely, Valerie Anderson Gaskill, Rosie Blunn, Andy Smith, James Telfor, Deborah Cunliffe, Jax Westmoreland, Helen Fitt, Connor MacLeod, Tudor Gwynn, Su Senior, Tess Hills, John Lusardi, Kath Thorpe, Tony Burger, Geneviève L. Walsh, Andrew Marsh, Cathy Bryant, Louise Fazackerley, Louella Ramsden, Caroline Sturges, Cathy Bryant, Marion Oxley, David Clegg, Derek Heine.*

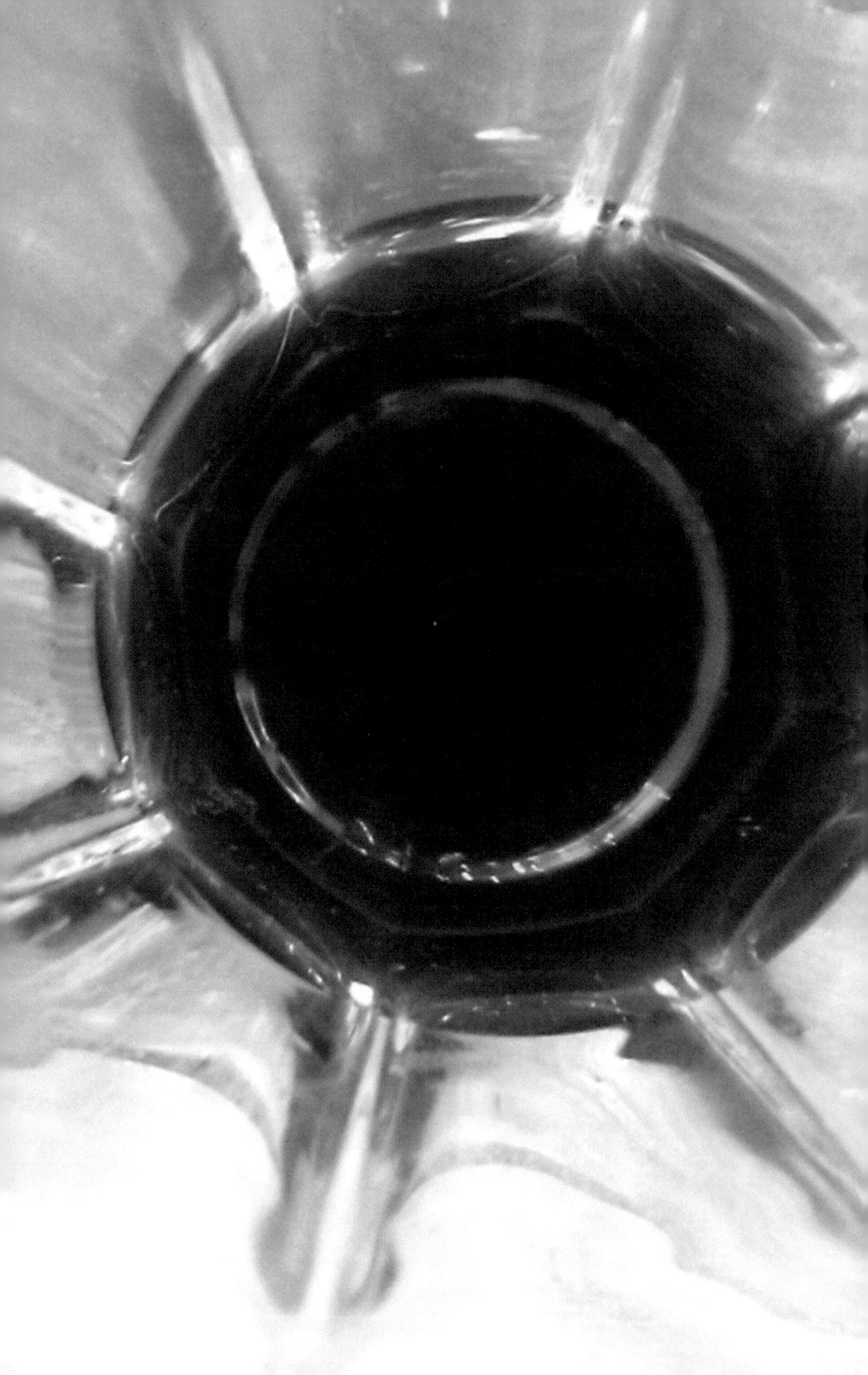

Park Life

The Coca-Cola Years

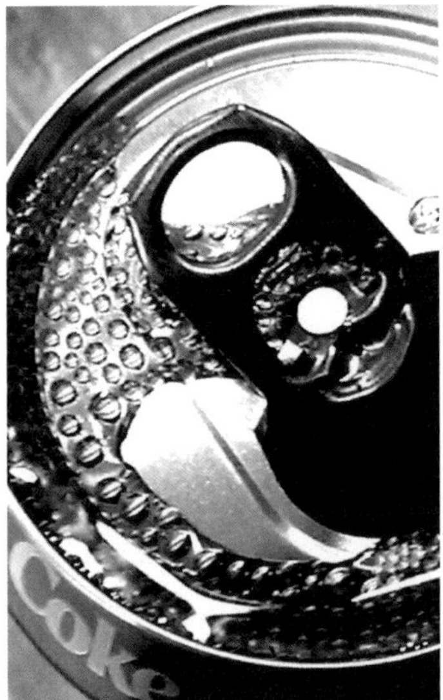

2

The following series of nine poems represent pareidolia poetry experiments, conducted by observing patterns on the surface of different varieties of Coca-Cola as it was poured into a highball glass. These patterns appear only fleetingly within the surface bubbles immediately after each pour. Great concentration is required to identify images that can be translated into poetry before they disappear. In some cases, reflections on the surface of the drink provided the stimulus, or the drink was swirled in the glass, casting a temporary pattern of bubbles on the glasses sides.

These poems were commissioned by Park Life Café, Calder-Holmes Park, Hebden Bridge, and were all written on the premises. The texts and the cans the drinks were poured from appeared as an installation in the cafe in 2016.

Bibendum
Coca-Cola

3 balloons, *pour*

Disappearing Milky Way, *pour* [86]

A beard of iron filings like those made on a game where facial hair is created on a picture of a face using a magnetic stick, *pour*

Headphones, *pour*

A jellyfish, *pour*

A rocket blasting off, *pour*

Afro Hair, *pour*

A hand, fingers pointing top left, *pour*

Bibendum, *pour* [87]

Nothing, pour

Nothing, pour

Nothing, pour

Nothing, pour

Nothing, pour

Pour

Drink.

Scots Pine Distortions
Coca-Cola

Skies clearing from the east, *pour*
Nothing, pour
A golden Halo, *pour*
Telephone with cord, *pour*
A distorted diamond, *pour*
An ice hockey goaltender's mask, *pour*
Nothing, pour
Solitary Scots Pine
A pork chop, *pour*
Cross section of citrus fruit segments.

Baily's Beads

Vanilla Coca-Cola

Baily's beads, *pour* [88]
A bridal bouquet flying through the air, *pour*
Sip, nothing, pour
A very poorly defined map of the world, *pour*
An anticyclone, *pour* [89]
Nothing, pour
A knee length sock, *pour*
Nothing, pour
A cul-de-sac, *sip*, *pour* [90]
Nothing, pour
A mushroom from Super Mario, *sip*, *pour* [91]
Inverted ace of spades, *pour*
BrewDog logo, *pour* [82]
A figure, arms and legs stretched out
Drink.

The Flowers of Orion
Cherry Coca-Cola

Hula hoops, *pour*
Distorted Europe, *pour*
The constellation of Orion, *pour* [93]
Nothing, pour
Nothing, pour
Curtains blowing out of a partially opened window, *pour*
Freesias, *pour*
Nothing, pour
Bluebells, *pour*
A white horse, *pour*
Boomerang, *pour*
Nothing.

Halva Moon
Coca-Cola

Sideburns, *pour* [94]
Nothing, pour
Halva, *pour* [95]
A rather rounded heart, *pour*
The Ant Hill Mob's car, *pour* [96]
Starfish, *pour*
The flag of Pakistan, *pour*
Clouds drifting across a crescent moon, *pour*
Arabic script.

Picking the Cathedral's Locks

Coca-Cola

Pour, nothing, swirl

A no entry sign turned through 90 degrees

A large ball with two smaller satellite balls, *pour*

Sand, *pour*

The cross section through a Swiss roll, *pour*

Ram's horns, *pour*

Nothing, pour

Cathedral buttresses, *pour* [97]

Hurricane Katia, *pour* [98]

Lock picking, *pour*

Hunched shoulders, *pour*

The Greek letter epsilon, *swirl* [99]

A ceaselessly blinking eye

Crescent moon passing by viewed
through a partly opened car window.

Random Inflations
Coca-Cola Life

Pour, swirl
Spider
Bat-signal, *swirl* [100]
A hat on its side, *pour*
Nothing, swirl
Squid, *swirl*
World map
Wolf, *pour*
A bubble gum bubble popping, *pour*
Air bags, *pour*
A sequence from the online game 'Mice', *pour* [101]
Sheet ghost face.

Jointly *composed by the author and Maisy Howell*

F is for Teapot
Coca-Cola

Pour, nothing
Aerial view of a Sixties lampshade, *pour*
Rheumatism bracelet, *pour* [102]
A propeller appearing to rotate slowly backwards, *pour* [103]
Nothing, swirl, nothing, pour
An inconclusive ultrasound scan, *swirl*
Negative images of vapour trails, *pour*
Coral, *swirl*
Capital letter F
Teapot.

Formation Nº 6
Coca-Cola

A rail mounted gun, *pour*, *swirl*
Mirror image of the number 6, *pour*
Kangaroo, *pour*
Stratus cloud formations, *pour* [104]
A brown crescent moon, *pour*
Nothing, swirl
Section of an aeroplane's fuselage
Stereotypical theatrical curtains *pour*
Empty
Sparks from an angle grinder.

The Raised Eyebrow of Wilma Flintstone

Diet Coca-Cola

Two broad beans, *pour*
Cartoon style gust of wind, *pour*
A pair of fluorescent strip lights, *pour*
Nothing, pour
Mirror writing, *pour*
The sinking of The Pequod, *pour* [105]
Wilma Flintstone's hair, *pour* [106]
Nothing, pour
Norway, *swirl*
The very first signs of rain, *pour*
Solitary raised eyebrow, *pour*
Nothing.

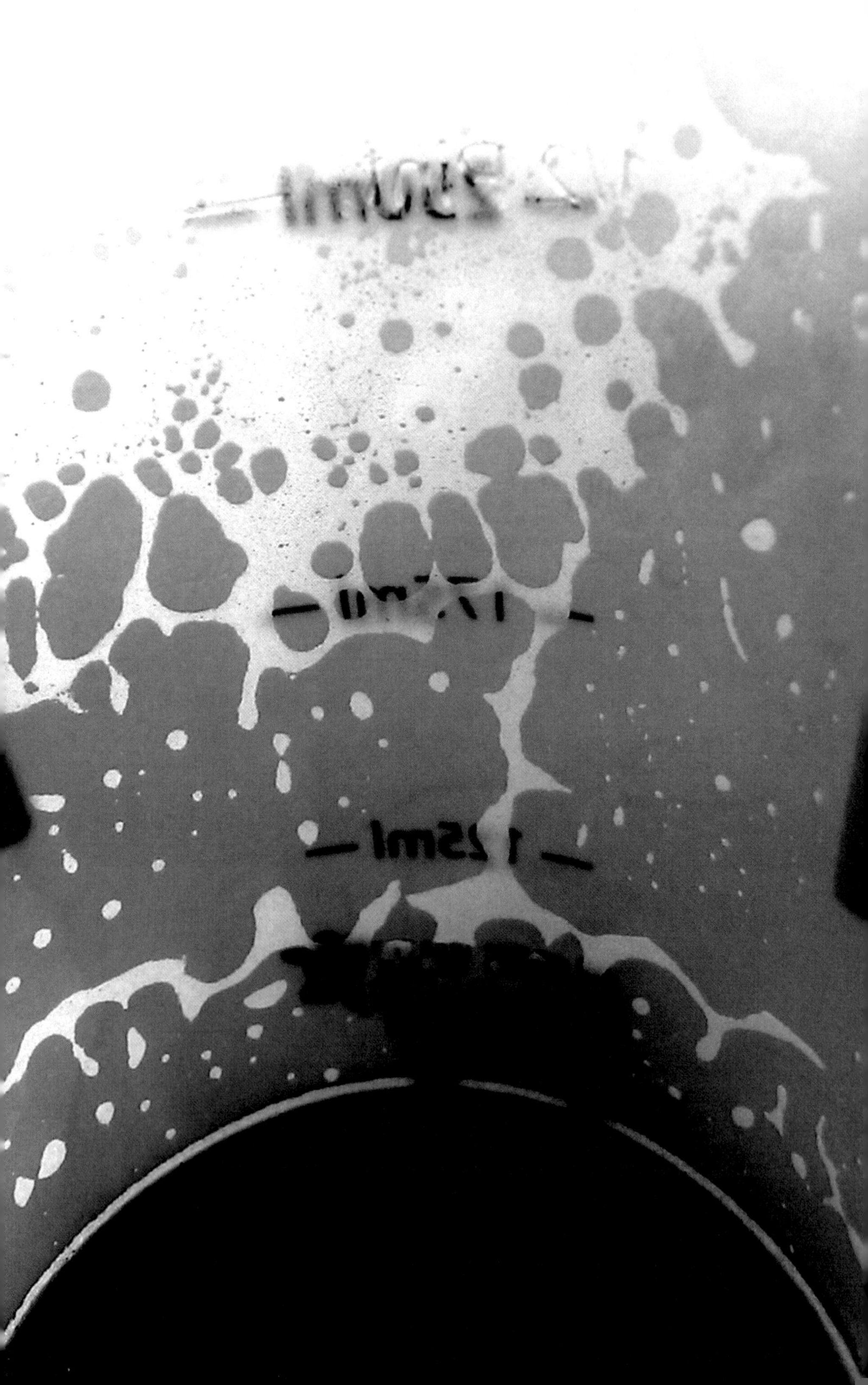

The Green Room
A Chronology

3

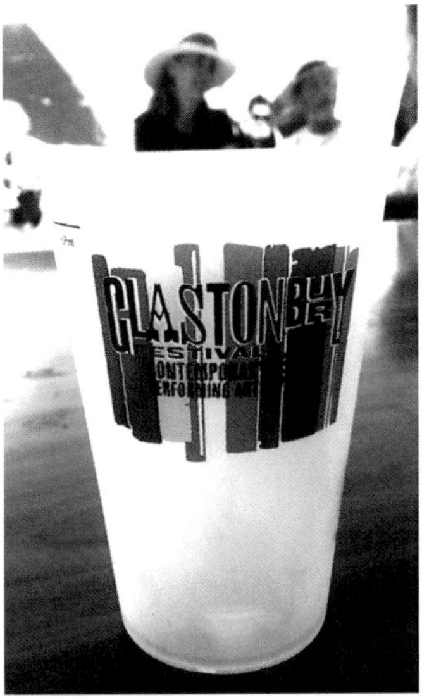

On a field trip to Glastonbury Festival of Contemporary Performing Arts 2015, the author, using a special festival edition plastic glass, collected half-pint samples of each of the six beers, produced especially for the festival by Glastonbury Microbrewery. Each was examined outside The Green Room Bar, in the back stage area of the Theatre & Circus field. The results that follow appear in chronological order from the first day of the festival to the last.

The Thought Fox [107]

Hedge Monkey

Traces of a fox, *sip*
Nothing, sip
Nothing, sip
Nothing, sip
Nothing
Nothing
Nothing.

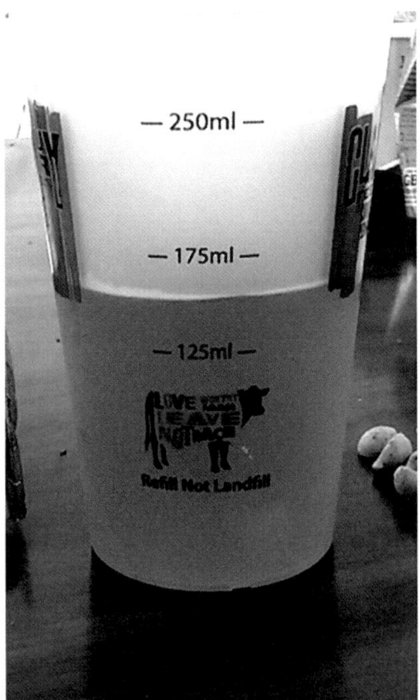

Surface of a glass of Hedge Monkey.

Petroleum Kisses

Pilton Pop

Sip

Chocolate kisses [108]

Face with a long thin nose, *sip*

A froglet, *sip* [109]

Tennis player at full stretch

A dragon sniffing the ground, *sip*

Petrol pumps, *sip*

A creature with many legs and large club-like feet, *sip*

A saxophone, *sip*

Empty.

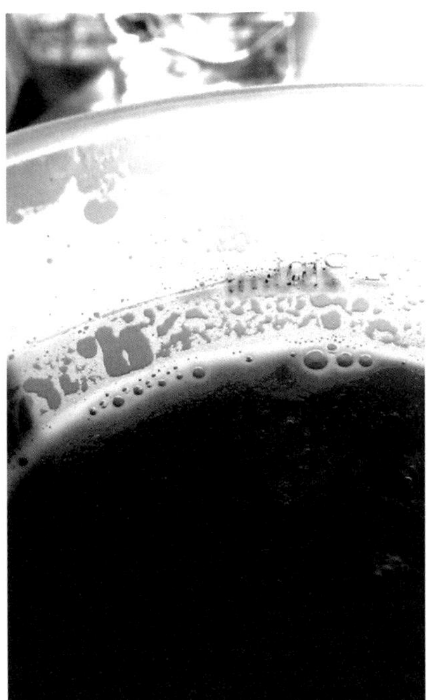

Sides of a glass of Pilton Pop.

The Last Flake of Snow on Middle Earth

Golden Chalice

Cherub, *sip*
Constellation of the Great Bear, *sip* [110]
Face of The Witch Lord of Angmar, *sip* [111]
Mist, *sip*
Knee (with part of calf and thigh)
Falling snow, *sip*
Nothing, sip
Nothing, sip
Nothing.

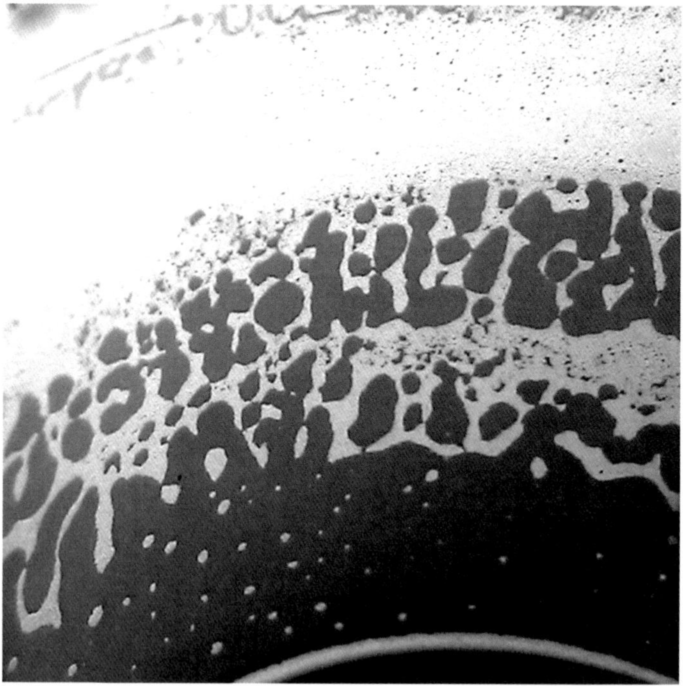

Surface and sides of a glass of Golden Chalice.

A Crooked Smile on Mount Rushmore

Dark As Yer' At

Face of a wolf, *sip*
Bart Simpson hair, *sip*
Mount Rushmore, *sip* [112]
Snake monster (with fangs), *sip*
A left footprint, *sip*
A crooked smile.

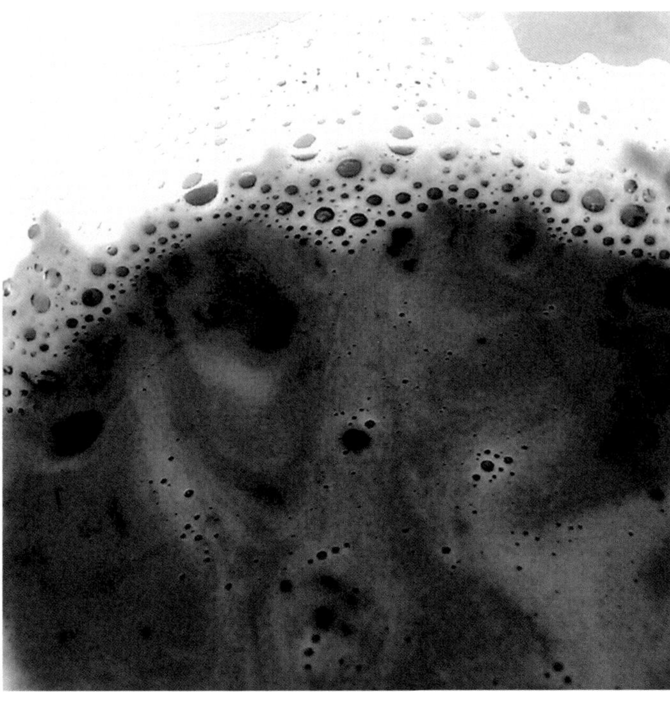

Surface and sides of a glass of Dark As Yer' At.

Spiv Bomb
Mystery Tor

A skull, *sip*
A question mark, *sip*
Fall out from an atom bomb detonation
Spiv moustache, *sip* [113]
Cartoon dog bone, *sip*
A gazelle running, *sip*
A reclining figure, *sip.*

Surface and sides of a glass of Mystery Tor.

The White Rainbow

Lady of the Lake

Sip

Tiger Stripes, *sip*

Dragon's fire, *sip*

A Gerald Scarfe doodle, *sip* [114]

White rainbow, *sip*

Metal frame of a plastic chair
commonly found in schools.

Surface and sides of a glass of Lady of the Lake.

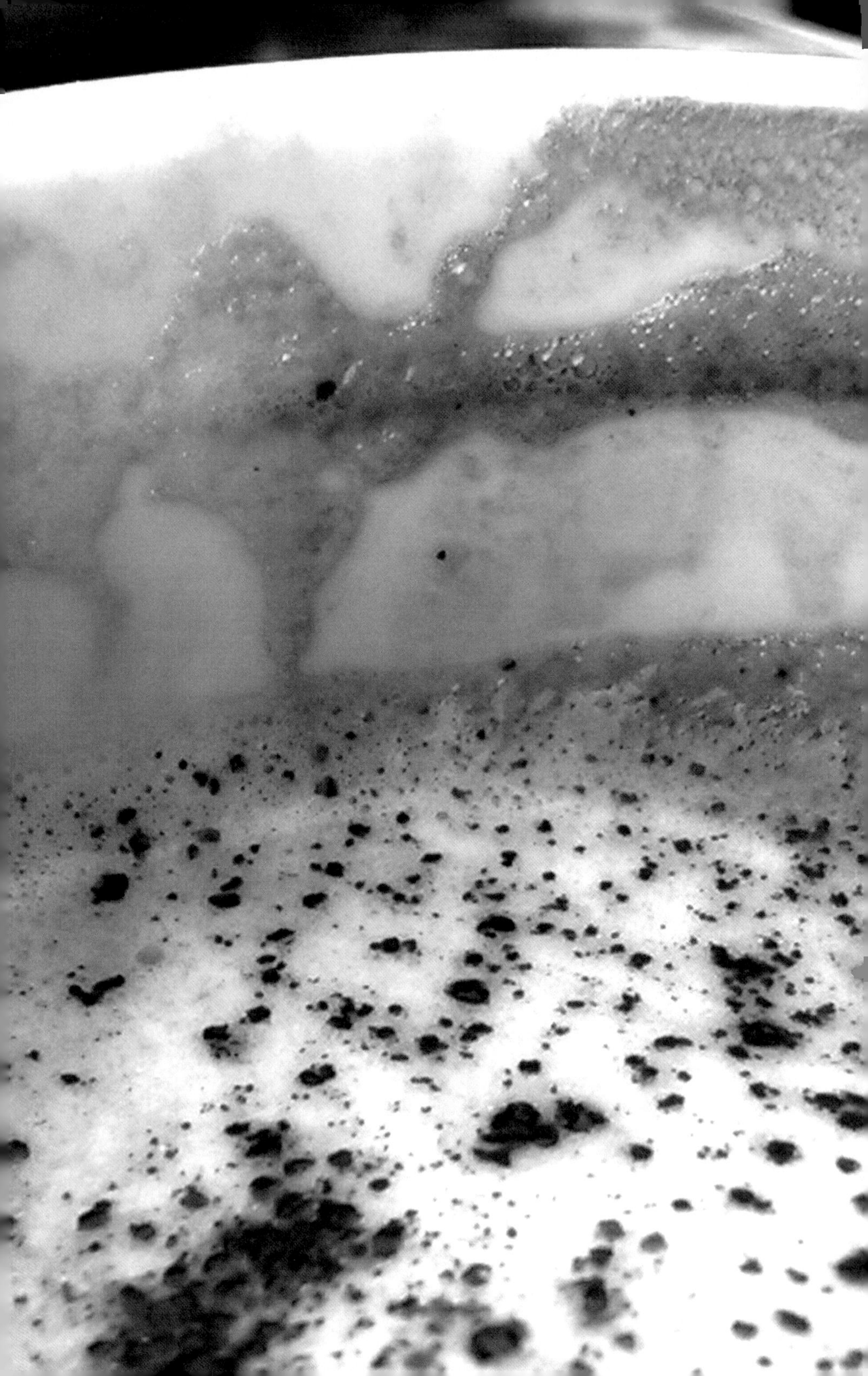

4

Java Lounge

In the Wake of the Wonderful Bean

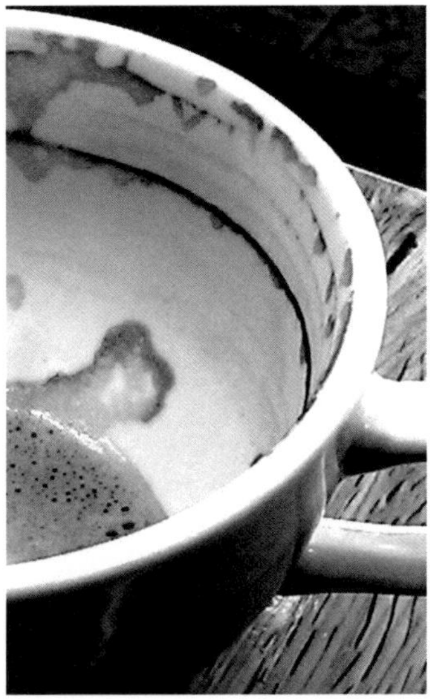

Welcome to the Java Lounge. Here you can enjoy the after effects of the wonderful bean. The echoing imagery rescued from left-over cups of hot chocolate and coffee usually photographed after the drinkers have left.

The last three entries in this section, (*pages 68-70*), represent an Anglo-American mini collaboration between myself and Texan poet Laurie Kolp. In composing them we allowed ourselves a less constrained editorial hand just because it seemed the natural thing to do. These three poems are therefore more cohesive and tread a more conventional path that those in the rest of this book.

(No beverages were consumed by the author in the composing of this chapter. His lifelong coffee consumption still remains at 13 cups).

One lump or two?

Enjoy…

Coppice on the Skyline

Found Latte

A roaring hare
Biology class drawing of fallopian tubes
A dog chew
Everest [115]
A coppice on the skyline
Moon craters
An obese rabbit
A man scratching his head
A rhinoceros.

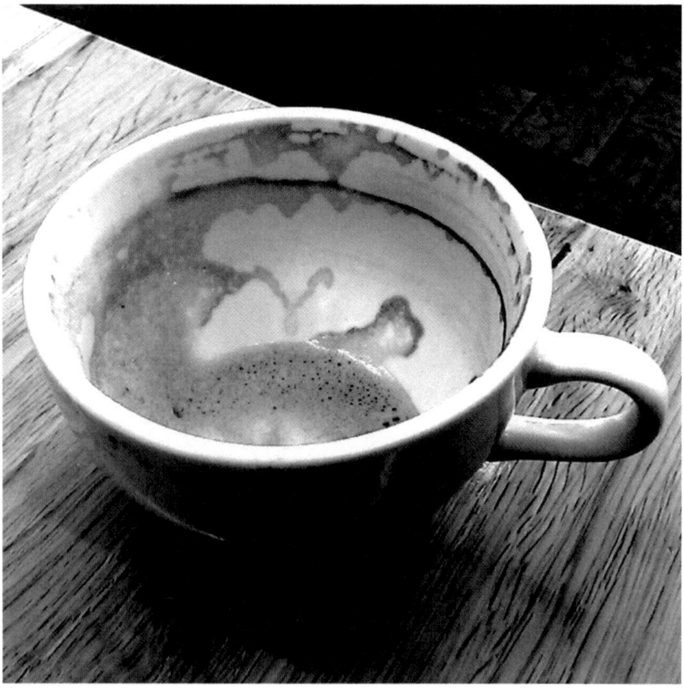

Empty discarded cup of latte.
Shibden Mereside Café, Shibden Park, Halifax.

Jointly *composed with Gaia Holmes*

The Eye of a Whale
Black Americano

A Grimm's fairytale, *stir* [116]
Spiral arm galaxy, *stir* [117]
Lightning tree, *stir*
An eye, *stir*
Mermaid, *stir*
Seal, *stir*
Whale, *stir*
The Scream of Nature by Edvard Munch, *stir* [45]
Hedgerows on the horizon, *stir*
A Chinese dragon, *stir*. [118]

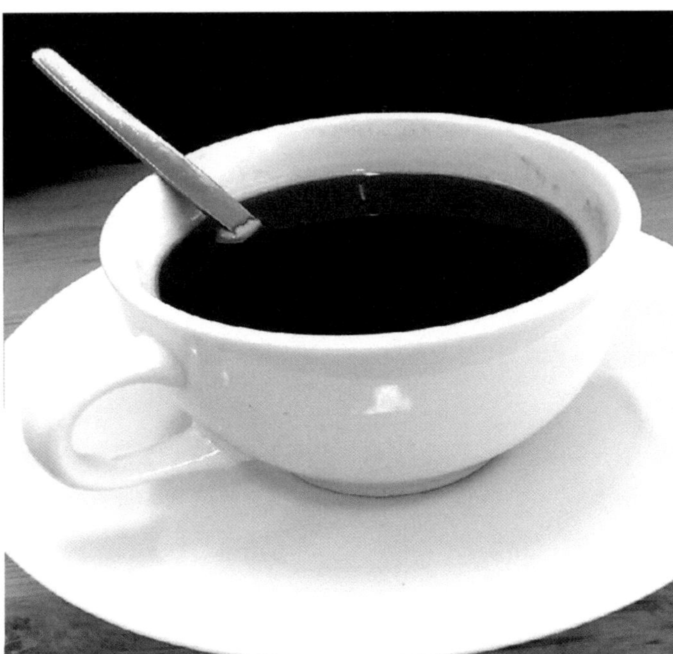

Surface of a cup of black Americano coffee after each stir.
Shibden Mereside Café, Shibden Park, Halifax.

Jointly *composed with Gaia Holmes*

The Curious Incident of the Dog in the Night-Time [119]

Flat White

Figures from a substitution cipher of dancing men [120]
A wobbly train with stream travelling through the night
A chaotic game of volleyball
An exploding bee
Dancing poodle
Demented Saint Bernard [121]
Hare looking left
A boxing hare
A headless bear spinning a teapot
on the claws of its right hand
Lazy mermaid.

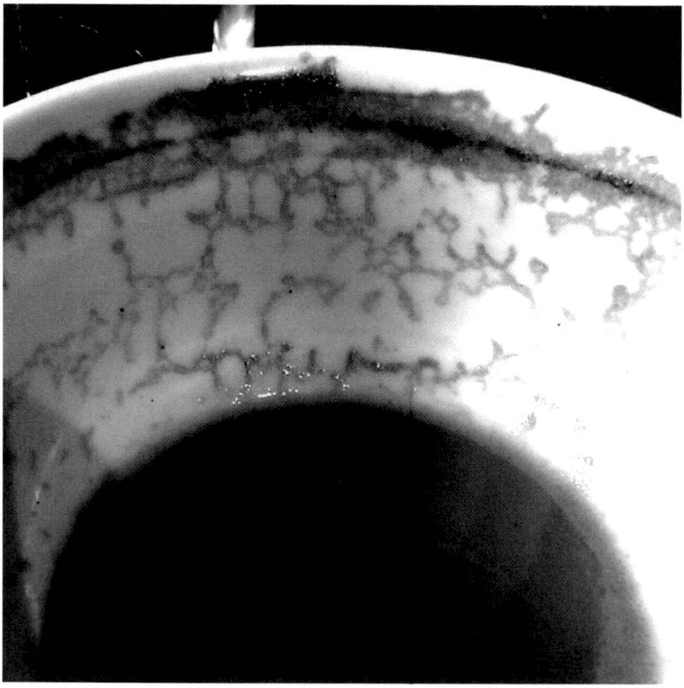

Empty cup of flat white.
Organic House Café, Hebden Bridge.

Jointly *composed with Maisy Howell*

Shadows of Space

Mocha

Scabs on lips

A dove

Cauliflower cloud formations

The vague outline of a man

Shadow of a cat

Space gun

Love heart shaped piece of ice,
separating from larger ice sheet

A swimmer

Images of the moons surface from the lunar lander [122]

A guitar on its side.

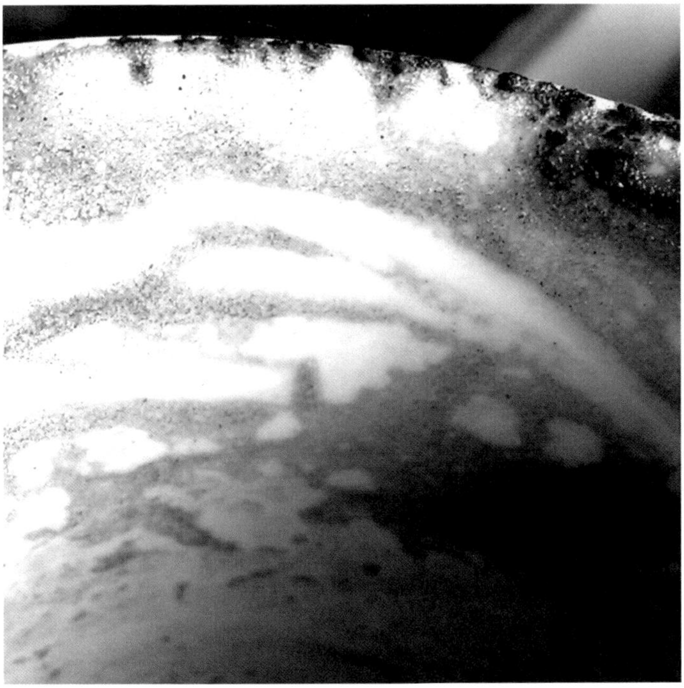

Empty cup of mocha.
Organic House Café, Hebden Bridge.

Jointly *and independently composed with Maisy Howell*

Three Wishes for The Hoff

Flat White

David Hasselhoff [123]
A teapot
U-boat about to surface [124]
Organ pipes in glass
Ice Hotel
Panning for gold
Aladdin style lamp
The lights from divers surfacing on a night dive.

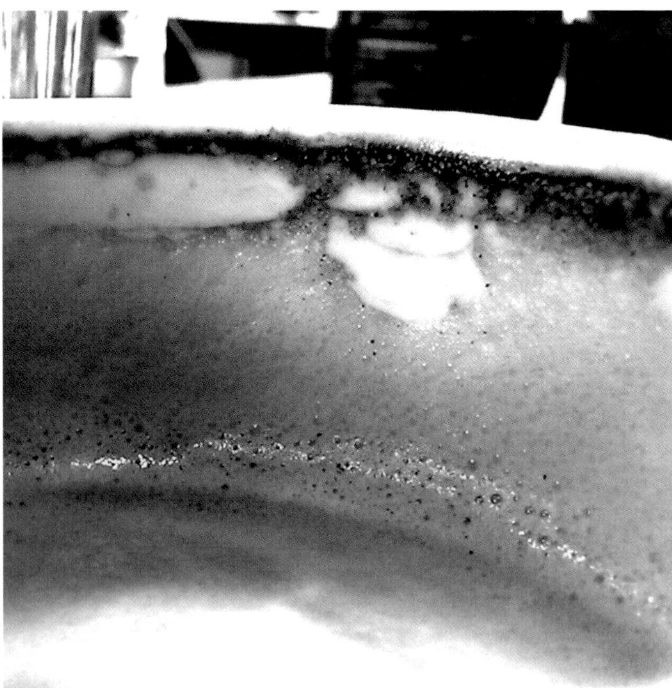

Found empty cup of flat white coffee and reflections in an empty highball glass. Park Life Café, Hebden Bridge.

Dogs Only Dream in Black and White

Coffee Beans

Emptying the canal
Butterfly chasing a Chinese silk orb
Woman with long tied back brown hair and a moustache
A one eyed screaming Halloween pumpkin
Black toggle (unfastened)
White dog waiting for his favourite ball to land
Dream with bloody nose

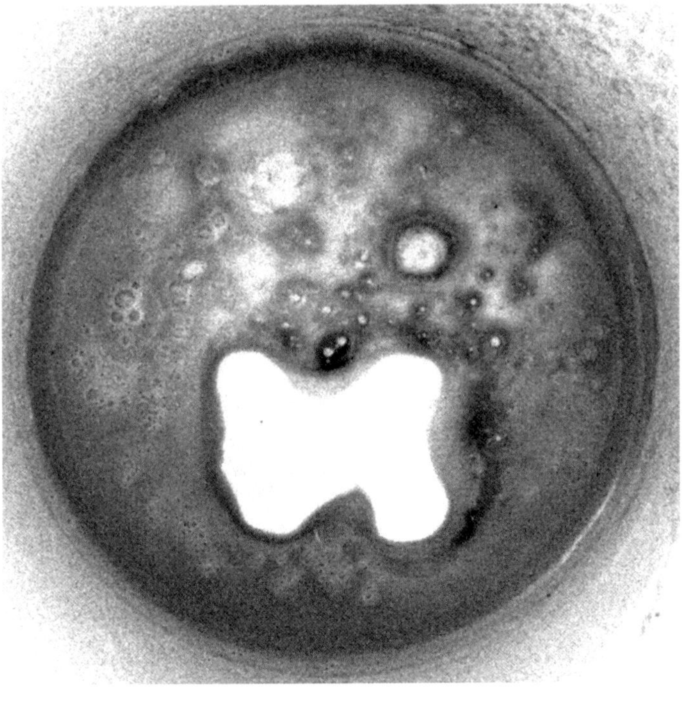

Latte sediment from home ground coffee beans.

Jointly *composed by the Author and Ruth-Robson-King*

Pearls of the Night Boatman

Coffee Beans

The man on the moon after a night on the tiles
Vinyl single with psychedelic record label [125]
A lamp lighter
Giant water boatmen [126]
A bubble blower
The collective intelligence of slime mold [127]
A child with two balloons
Footprints amongst a broken pearl necklace
A cucumber aspiring to be holey cheese.

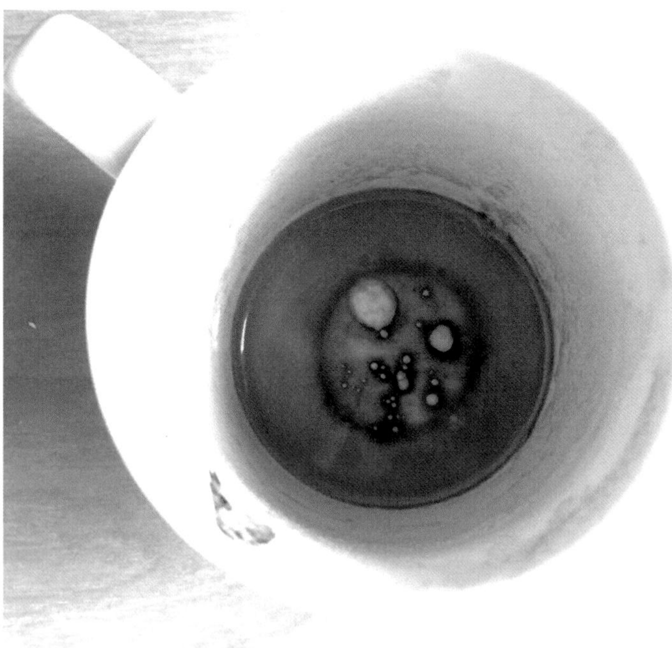

Latte sediment from home ground coffee beans.

Jointly *composed by the Author and Ruth-Robson-King*

Storm Door
Coffee Granules

Coalbunker with broken door
Coral reef in a storm
Driving through a moorland fire
Solar flares from a midnight sun
Autumn flurry
Stoker's eye view
Hell's trapdoor
Sharing a bonfire with my brother
Walking home along the cinder path at dusk

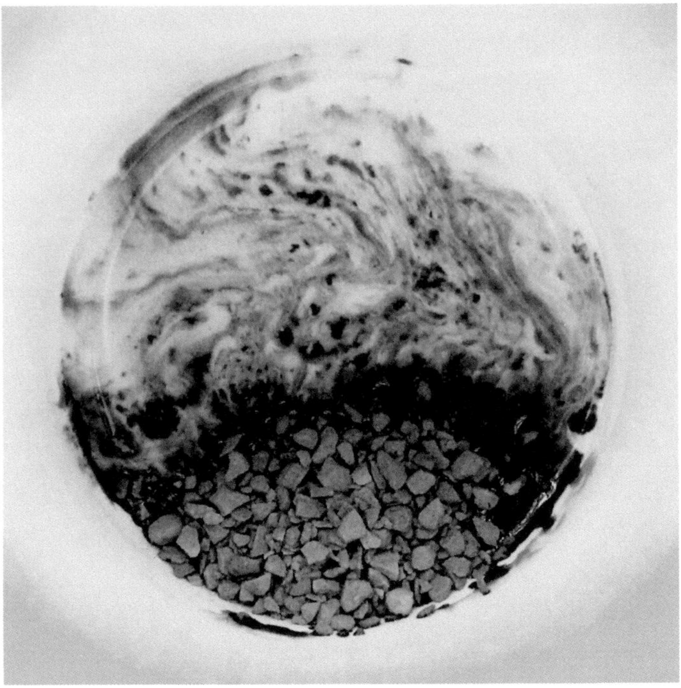

Instant coffee granules dropped into a wet cup.

Jointly *composed by the Author and Ruth-Robson-King*

Bent-kneed in Snow
Hot Chocolate

The Peloton d'exécution [128]
Track through the snow
A bent-kneed camel meets a row of ghosts
Two poodles sniffing a baby's elephant toy
Flakes sliding down windscreens.

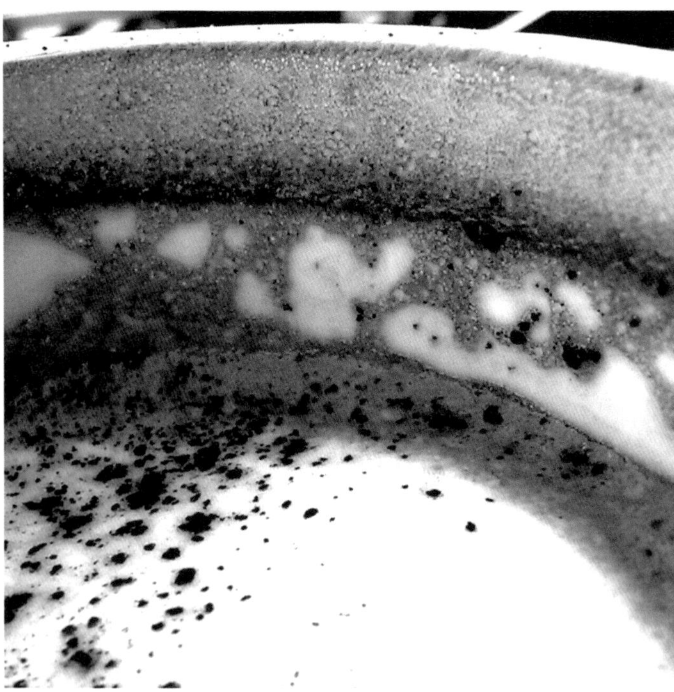

Sides of a half empty cup of hot chocolate.
Found at The Park Life Café, Hebden Bridge.

Lines *by Laurie Kolp and The Author, edited by the author.*

Dot in the Distance

Hot Chocolate

A sixties mountain landscape reflected in a lake
Knuckles swollen, fingers can't grasp anything
Argyle socks gathered at the calf [129]
I waved goodbye to you
My black sugar mouse.

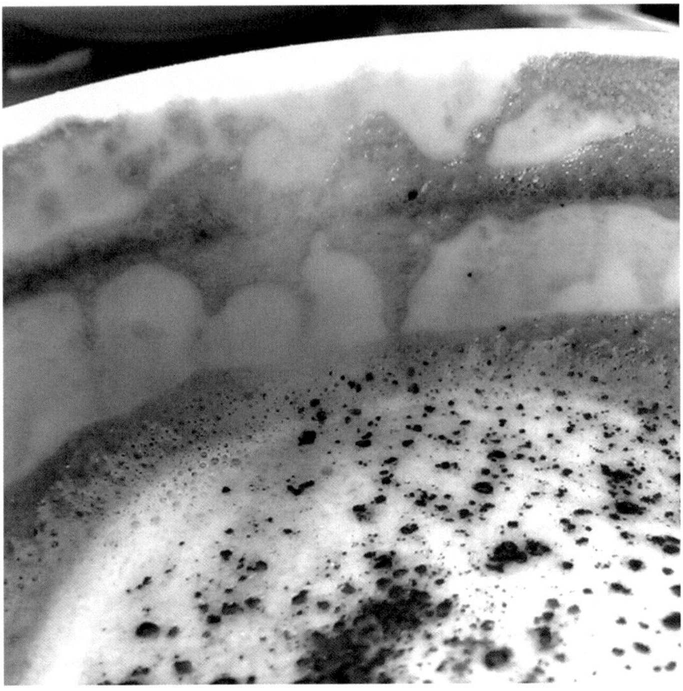

Sides of a half empty cup of hot chocolate.
Found at The Park Life Café, Hebden Bridge.

Lines *by Laurie Kolp and The Author, edited by the author*

The Empathy Trap

Unknown

A storm on a far off planet mirrored your shining eye
Blood white, turning away
The last rays of sun drift in space
Two hands touch and the storm ends.

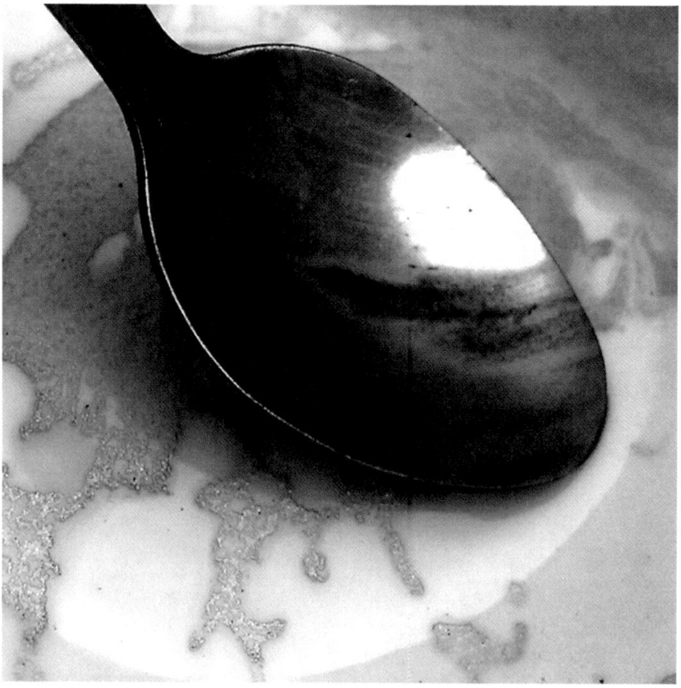

Sides of an empty cup of an unknown beverage with spoon.
Found at The Park Life Café, Hebden Bridge.

Lines *by Laurie Kolp and The Author, edited by the author*

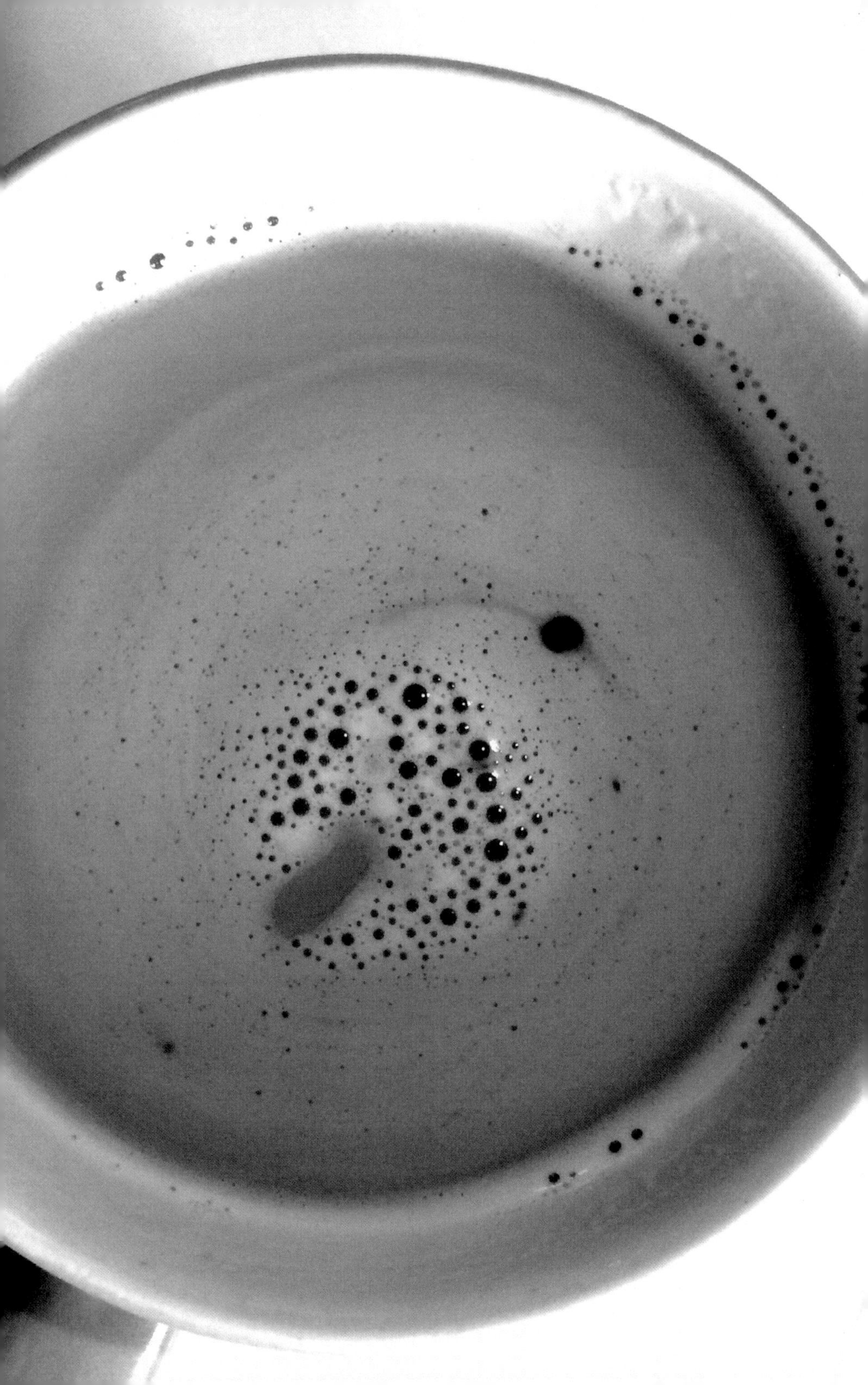

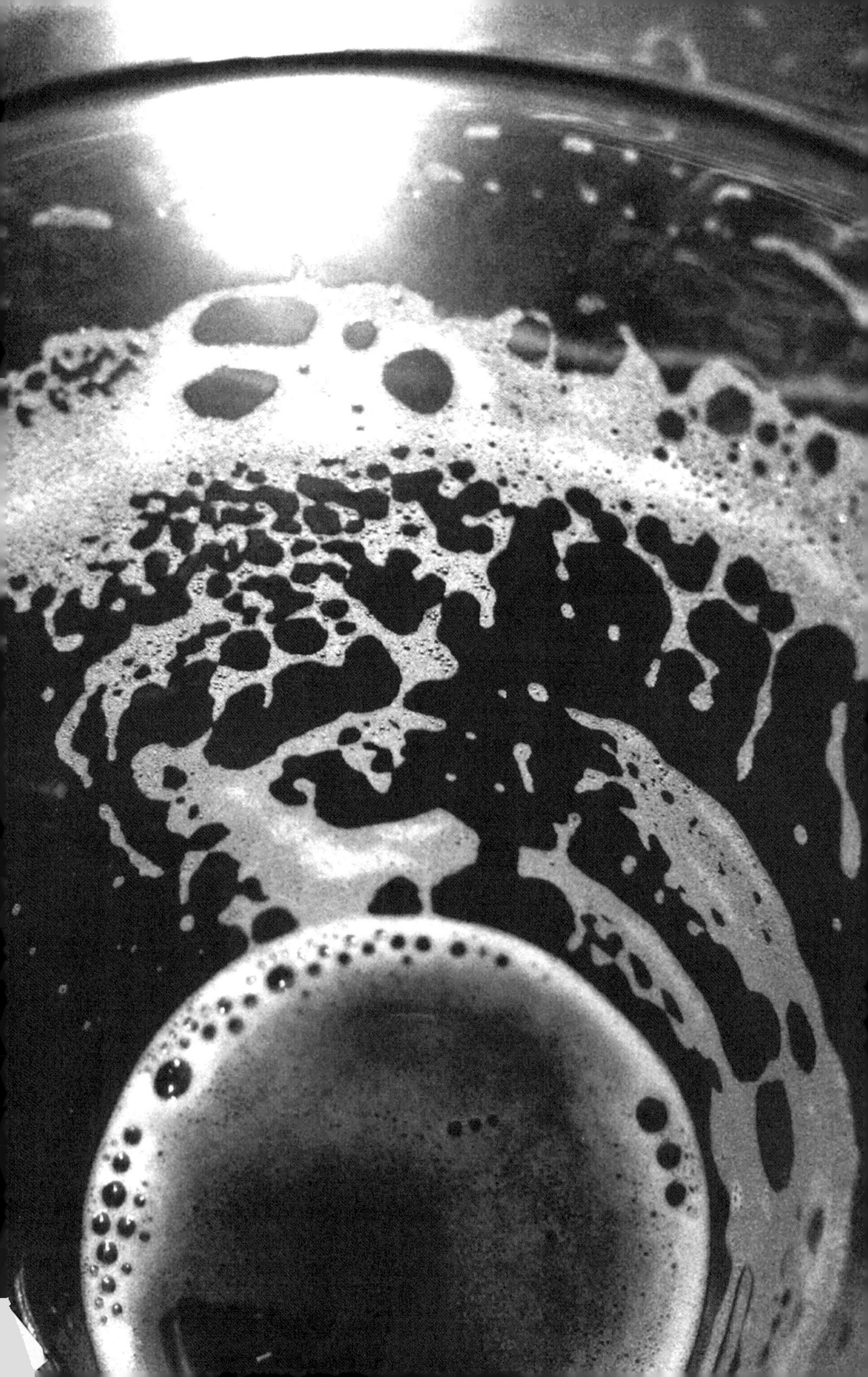

Beer is Good

Chinking Glasses Across the Pond

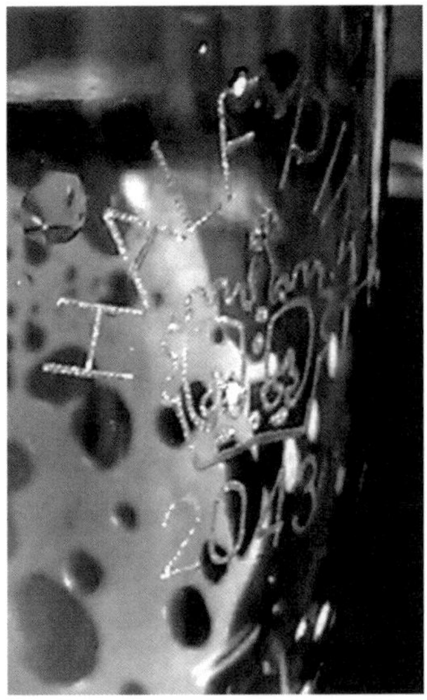

5

This section's poems were inspired by images sent over from Florida, where Pete Anderson and Jim Scortino run their own nano-brewery and pub. With a name like The Pareidolia Brewing Co., it would be remiss of me to overlook these fine ales in a book on this subject. Each of the nine poems derived from a photograph of a different beer is nine lines long.

> “*Most people see objects in clouds or religious figures in toast but you can see just about anything with a good imagination.*”

Pareidolia Brewing Co.,
Sebastian, Florida, United States.

PAREIDOLIA BREWING CO. ® FACE IT, BEER IS GOOD!

All images courtesy of Pete Anderson

Single Scoop Backdrop

Pass it Down

Martini in a conical glass with an olive on a stick
Hanglider with mountain backdrop
Gypsy headband of gold
!
Indian elephant
Mustard pot with spoon
Italy
Broken skull fragments
Single scoop cone of ice cream.

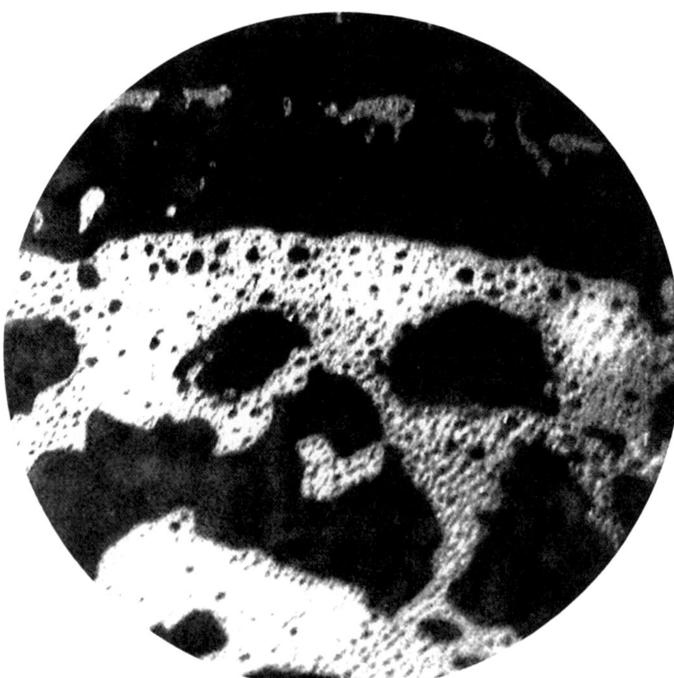

Pass it Down Porter.

Rabbit Unmasked

Sebastian

St Bernard with brandy barrel
Molar
Panda
Man stooping over a laptop
Masked eyes with fat lips
Muscle man
Rabbit riding a fat rocking horse
Noddy's car [130]
Figure hugging top.

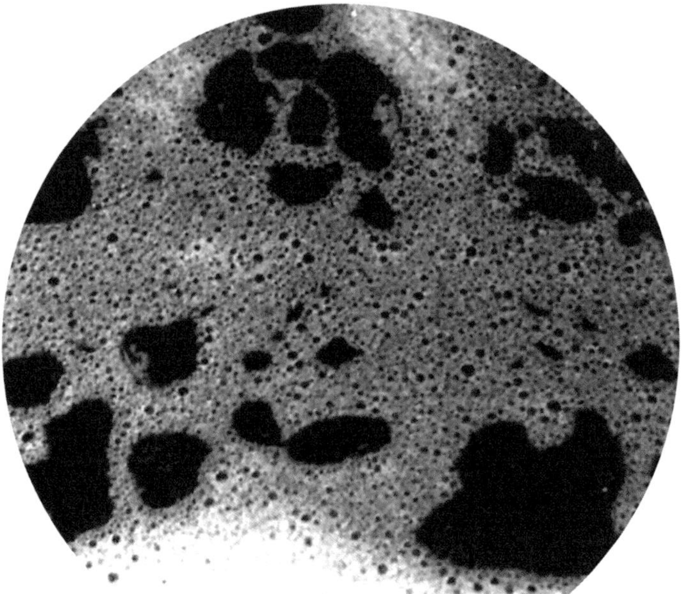

Sebastian Scottish Ale.

The Earth Was Born in a Pinball Machine

Peanut Butter Porter

Planet Earth from space
A seventh wave [131]
Bird skull
A jalapeño pepper [132]
Snow being blown from the edge of a cornice [133]
Ball in a pinball machine being launched [134]
Earless white rabbit sitting
Wavy reflection of a calabash pipe [135]
An object emerging on a Star Trek transporter platform. [136]

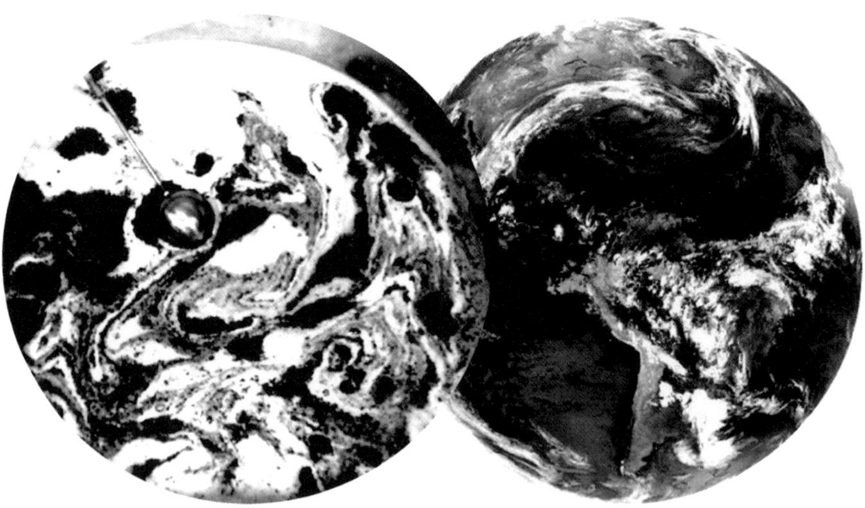

Photograph looking into the mash tun at the start of the brewing process of Pete's Peanut Butter Porter.
Left: Pareidolia Brewing Company's mash tun.
Right: Enhanced contrast greyscale image from NASA's Goddard Space flight of Earth on 31 December 2012.

Leaning on the Spade

Late in the Day

White rabbit looking right
Toad spawn
Spade from a child's seaside bucket and spade set
Leaf growing from a trunk with no branches
Friesian cow's head [137]
A running nose
Circular harbour with sea wall
An italic capital I, leaning the wrong way
Paw print with three toes.

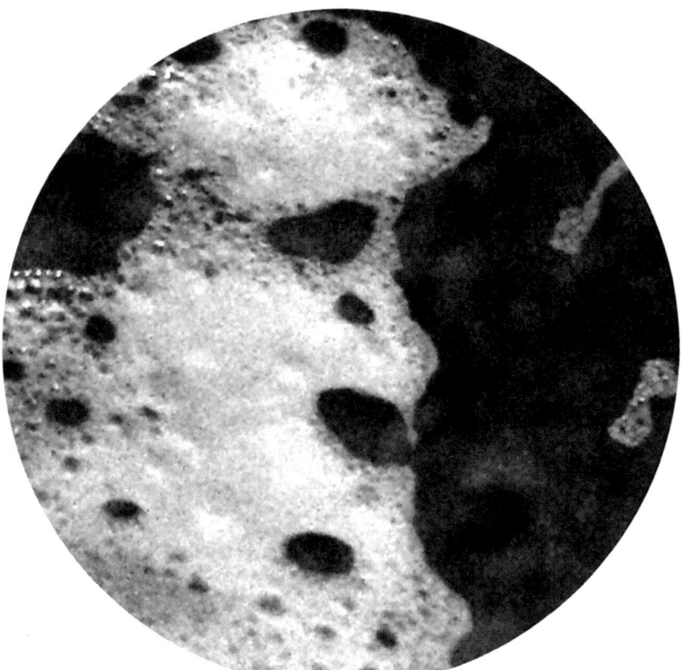

Late in the Day Amber Ale.

The Unexplored Face

The Duke

A porthole gathering condensation

Pleading monkey face showing teeth

Tunnelling

Seagull amongst the stars

The James Bond moon buggy (plan view) [138]

Compression stroke of an
internal combustion engine cylinder

Hair follicle

Unexplored nebulae [139]

Lathe swarf [140]

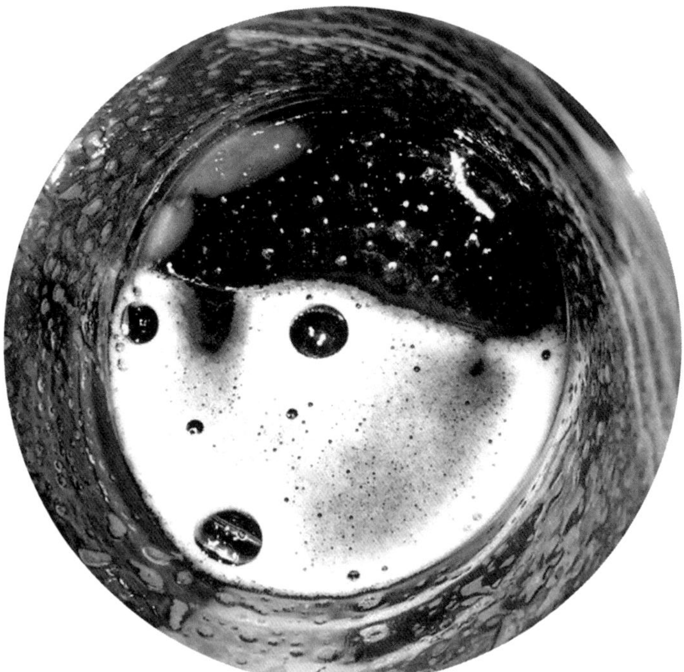

A glass of The Duke IPA.

Old Grey Mare

Red Ale

Elongated White Horse of Uffington [141]
Spider Man laughing [142]
The Watcher in the Water [143]
The Old Grey Whistle Test opening titles [144]
Two venomous snakes striking
Sprite throwing a spear
Miner at a coalface
Unidentified nostrils
A circular lemon meringue pie.

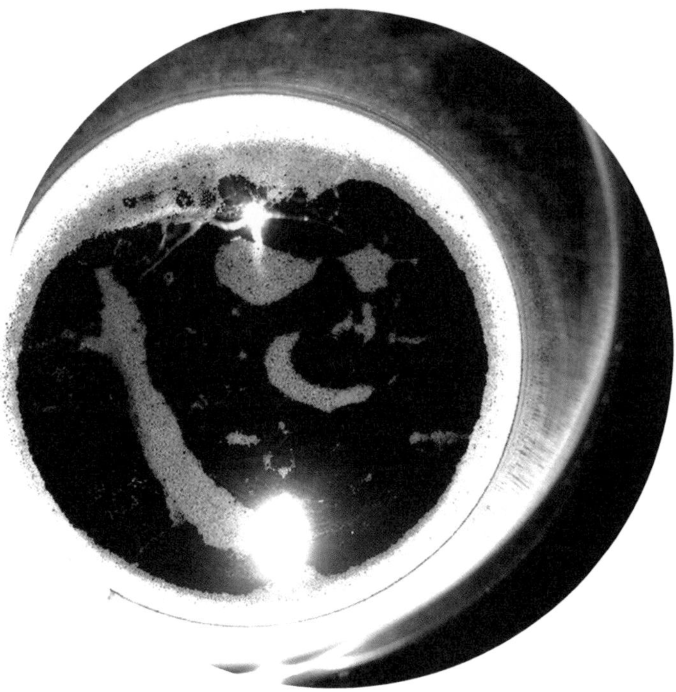

Right Point Red Ale.

Names on an Unlikely Guest List

Pareidolia Porter

Croctopus [145]
Figure dancing in the rain
Bass clef and staves with unrecognisable notes
Steam train
Gathering storm clouds the colour and texture of Baileys [146]
Ghost party
A skipping figure with an enormous hole in torso
Gawping monkey
Vacant expression wearing a beret. [147]

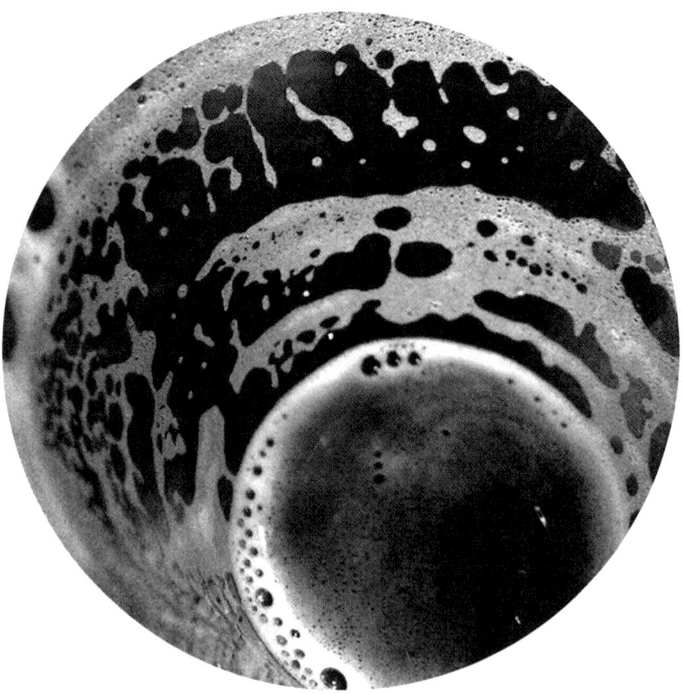

A glass of Pareidolia Porter.

Under the Bark of Life

In Da Cat

Lip of a pitcher plants trap [148]
Cookie Monster eating cookies [149]
Sneezing anteater
Spider's eyes
A Clanger [150]
Compass needle pointing southeast
Early life forms
Black jumper left on the floor overnight
Under the bark of driftwood.

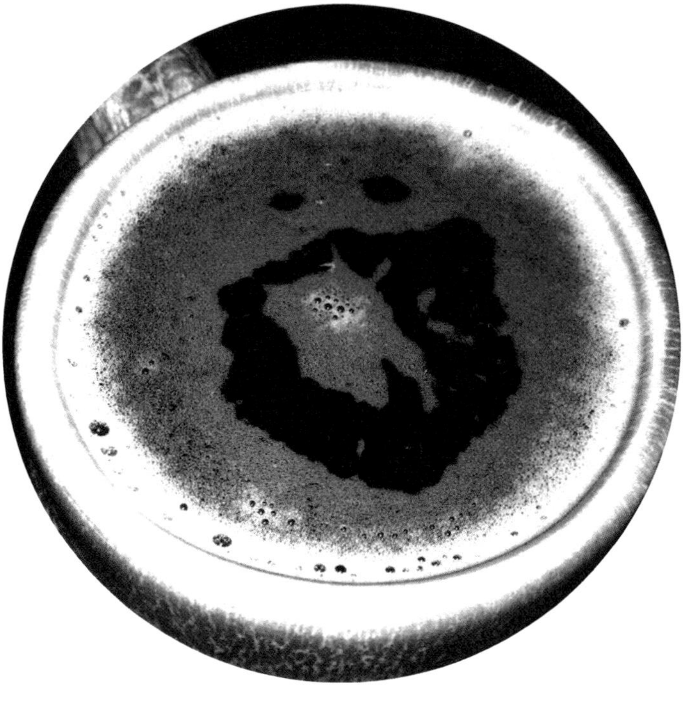

Surface of a ceramic tankard of In Da Cat Pale Ale.

Hopeful Monsters [151]

YRUSO Pale Ale

Aerial view of a base jumper about to deploy parachute [152]

A sudden ray of hope

Y-Fronts

A wind-up kiwi with cloak trailing in the wind

Beginners guide to acrobatics for monsters

Car steering wheel

The magic door appearing in The North Face of the Eiger [153]

Storm cloud discharging

Copper sheet with verdigris. [154]

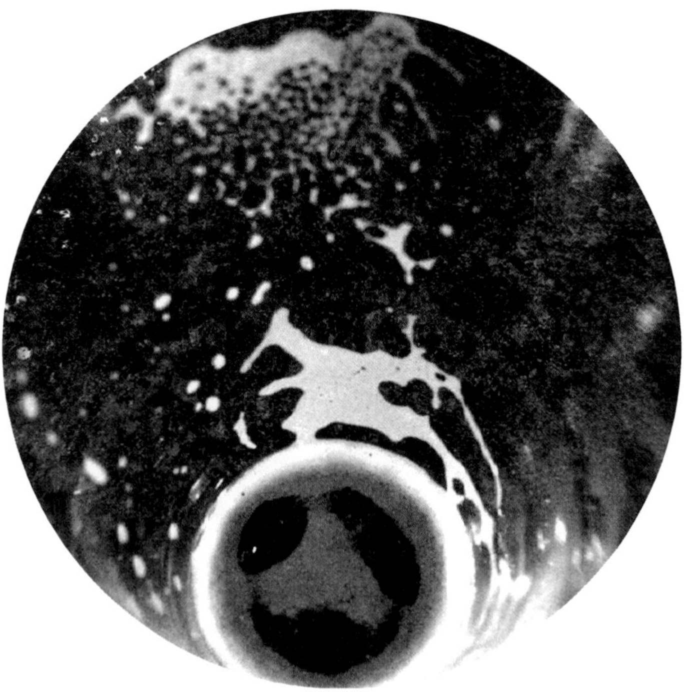

YRUSO Pale Ale.

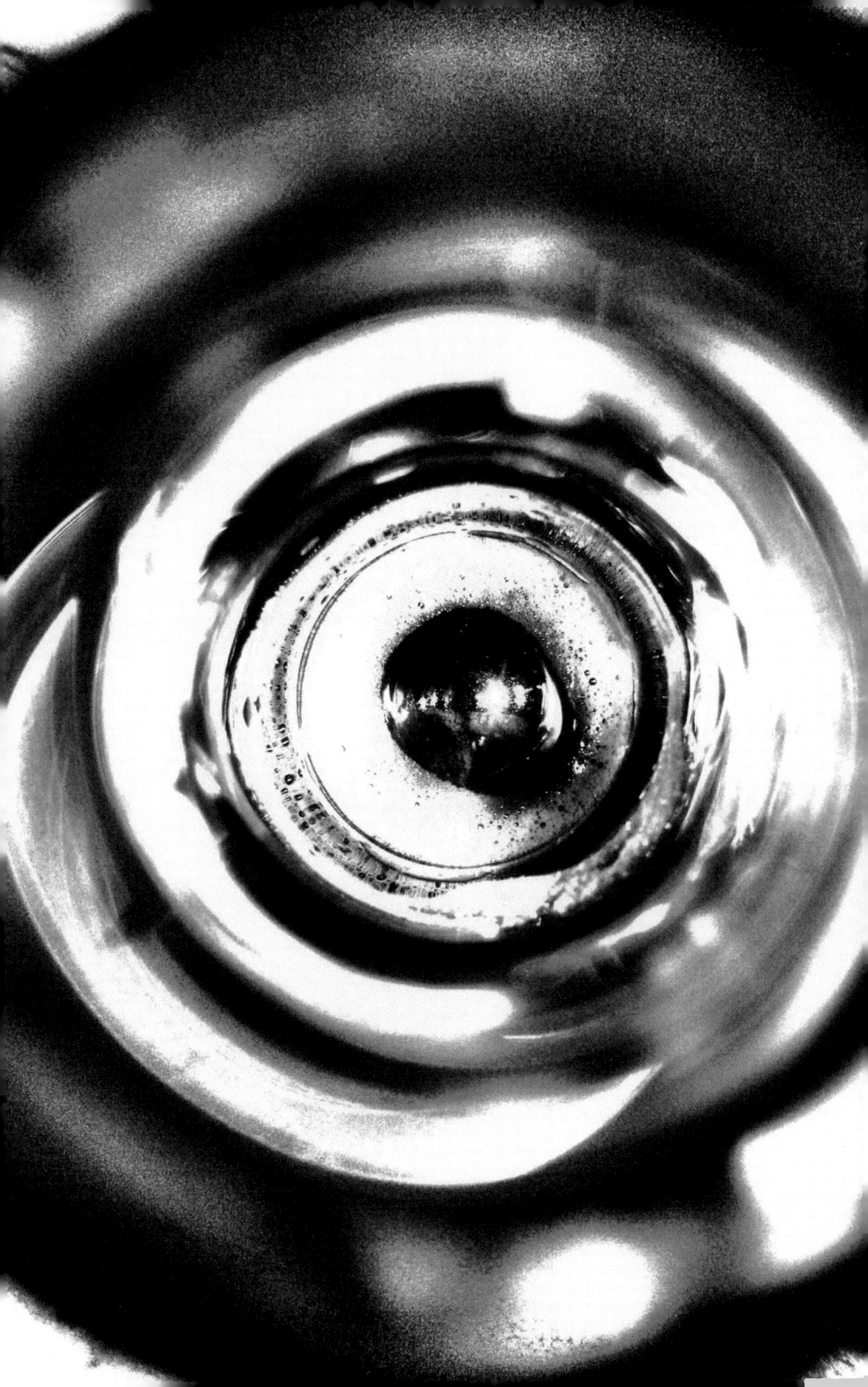

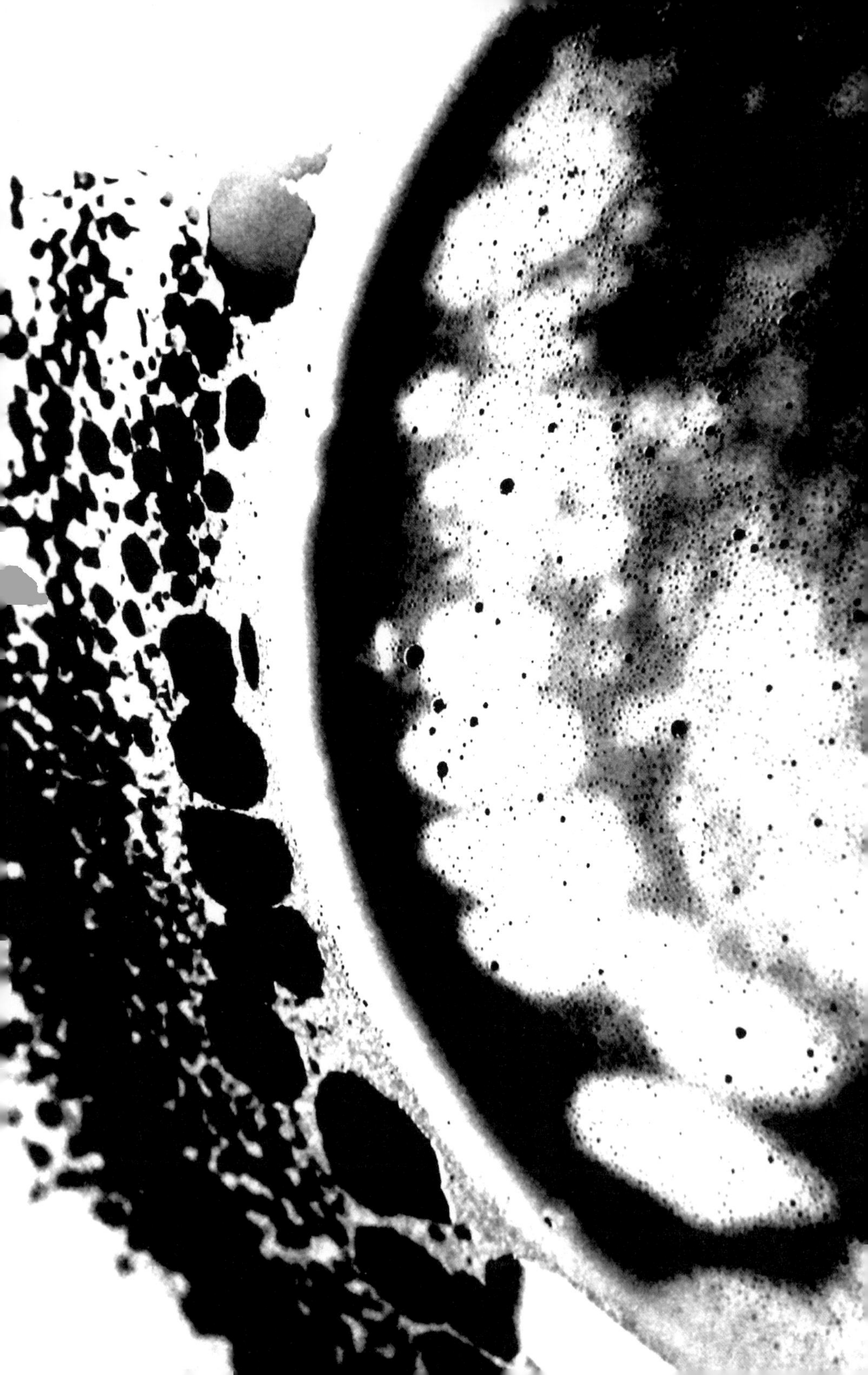

6

Monochrome Alternations

Two Men's Musings

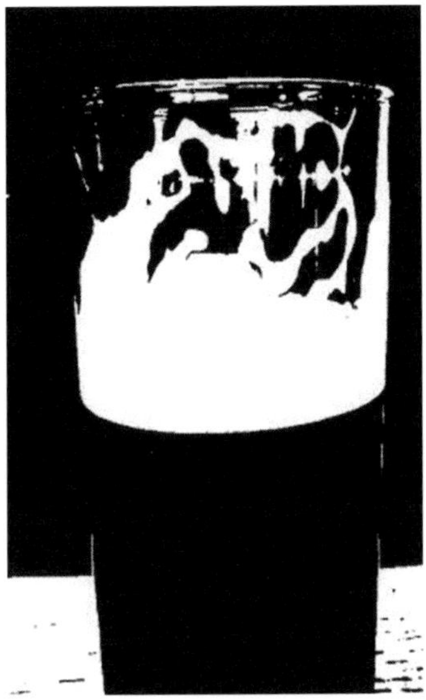

The following collection represents a collaboration between the author and Mytholmroyd artist Jason Howgate.

The writing process was conducted entirely by online observation via private message on Facebook, from photographs taken by the author. Originally in colour, the images have been digitally rendered in black and white with all greyscale removed.

Messrs Plowes and Howgate composed all lines remotely and independently, these lines being later interlaced to form poems of lines alternating between writers. Any perceived narrative or repeated imagery from line to line is therefore purely a matter of chance.

Note – *JH* or *WP* indicates which author's line came first in the footnotes on each page.

Invasion of the Alien Bees

Bengali

Melting ice flow in the Arctic

Solar Flares

Frankenstein (lonely figure) [155]

Five juggling clubs in a cascade [156]

Alien spacecraft moving through the galaxy preparing to invade

Sloth reaching upwards

Grumpy cartoon monster being attacked by bees

Paintbrush icon.

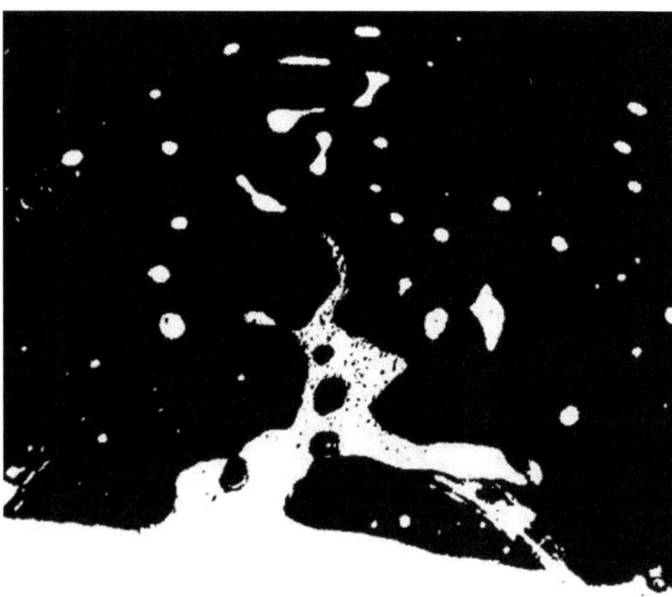

Sides of a glass of Sixpoint Craft Ales Bengali IPA.
Table 35, The Percy Shaw, Halifax. *JH*

Floodlit Autopsy

Hooky Gold

A white hedge trimmer and falling cuttings
Bereft Beelzeboul [157]
Rabbit with a club
Pop art lion [158]
Irises
Love heart vegetation
Puffer fish (inflated)
The Master and Magarita [159]
Profile of teeth from an advert about gum disease
A floodlit Buddhist temple
Zygon autopsy [160]
Hangover beer demon.

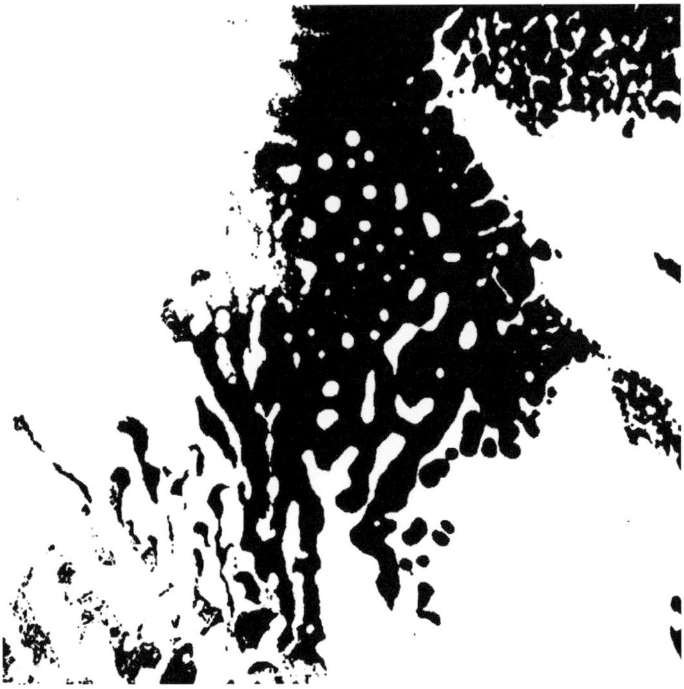

Sides of a pint glass of Hook Norton, Hookey Gold.
The Works, Sowerby Bridge. *WP*.

Carnival of the Animals [161]

Pentland

A fish fin trailing foam
Saltwater crocodile off Cornwall [162]
Evil hand shadow (left in White)
Pollen falling from a flower
Old Mother Shipton (right in black) [163]
David Hockney's sinister splash [164]
A tent half way up a mountain
Otter escaping from a zoo
Cuttlefish bone
Whale sperm.

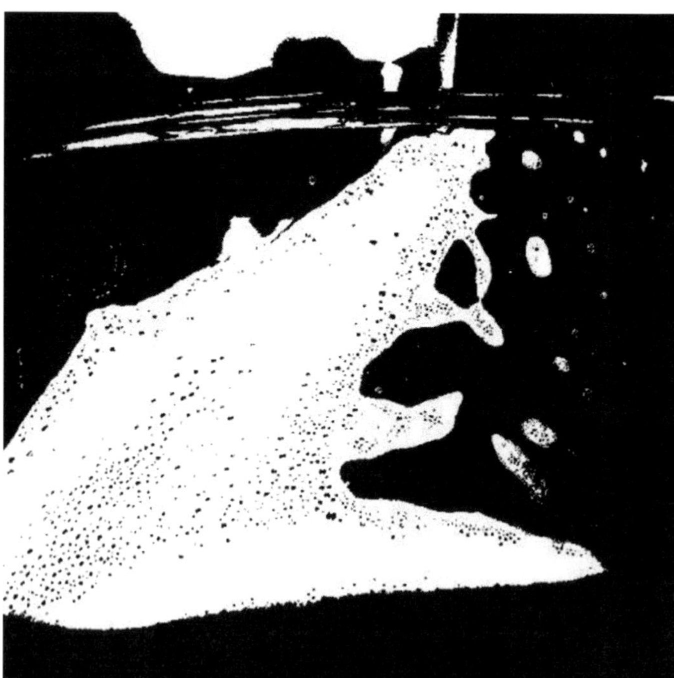

Sides of a half-pint glass of Stewart Brewing, Pentland IPA.
The Flotterstone Inn, near Penicuik, Midlothian. *WP.*

Space Cowboy

Landlord

Tarantula on a desert island
Space cat
Rosy-cheeked celestial eclipse
Alien air strike from space weapons
Paint splatter on a backstreet wall
Balloon dog with a deflating tail
Silhouette of a bucket tulip
Solitary Christmas tree in the snow
View obscured by a cowboy hat
Ying Yang backwards writing
Archerfish missing its prey. [165]

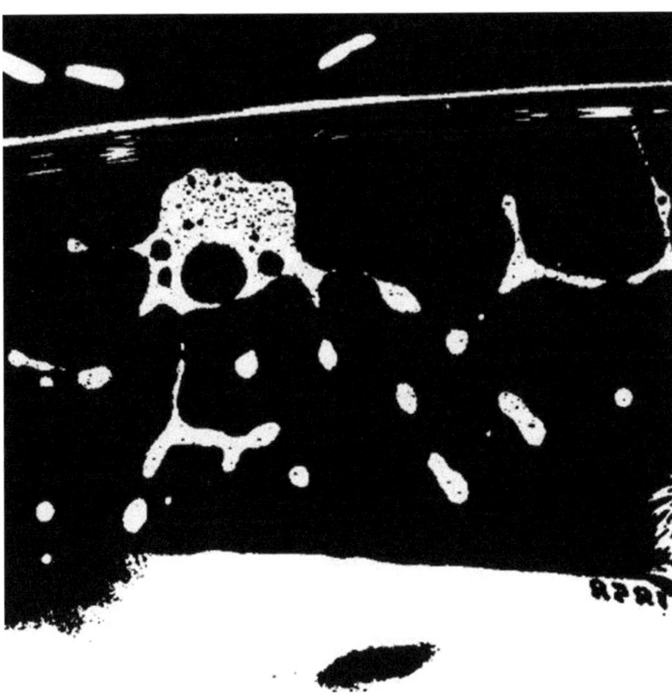

Sides of a half-pint glass of Timothy Taylor's Landlord.
The Works, Sowerby Bridge. *JH.*

Tales from the Land of Nod

XP

Echo sounding for shipwrecks
Homer rests in peace
The surfacing tail of Moby Dick [166]
Heath Robinson contraptions [167]
A Lee-Enfield rifle [168]
Scrimshaw [169]
Rubber duck
Steam liner keeling over
Eskimo fishing hole
Land of Nod. [170]

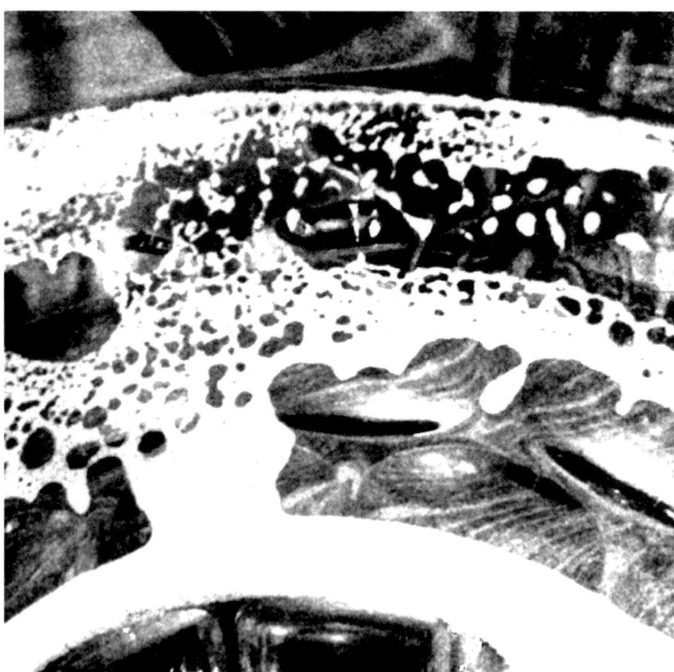

Sides of a half-pint glass of The Hop Studio's XP.
The Fox and Goose, Hebden Bridge. *WP.*

Perseus Entombed

Old Speckled Hen

Tyres crunching past a puddle
Five ghost chicks chatting
British 1950's wool textiles
Psychedelic stamp perforations
RED MEN
60's oil wheel projection [171]
Aboriginal cave drawing [172]
Multiball volleyball
August meteor showers over the island [173]
Wilson, Keppel and Betty [174]
Nebulous figure happily entombed
A worn brake disk.

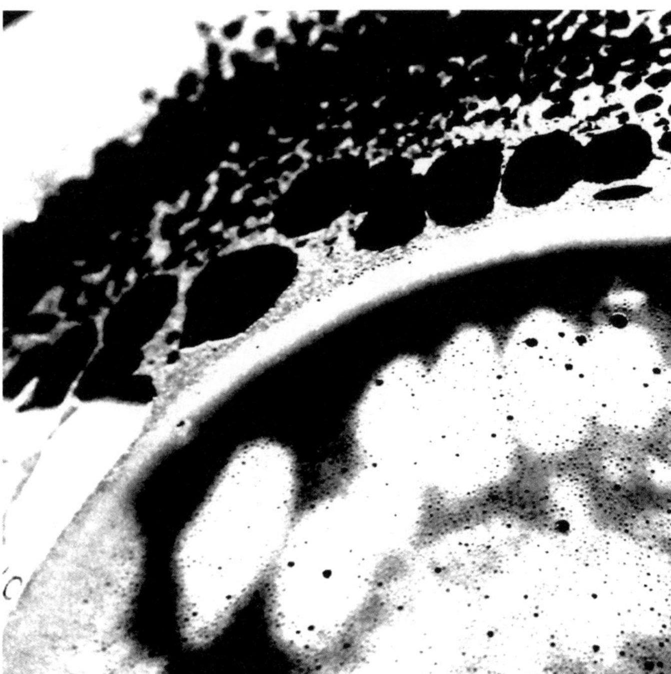

Sides of a glass of Greene King / Morland Brewery
Old Speckled Hen. At home (poured from a can). *JH.*

Je t'aime
Cocker Hoop

Fertilisation

Psycho Shower [175]

Swimming goggles

"Every time it rains, it rains pennies from heaven" [176]

Romanesque head with top half of skull sliced off [177]

Je t'aime Gitane [178]

Happy octopus

Toilet scum slidings

Religious iconographic figure in black
with a jalebi necklace [179]

Lichens on tree bark. [180]

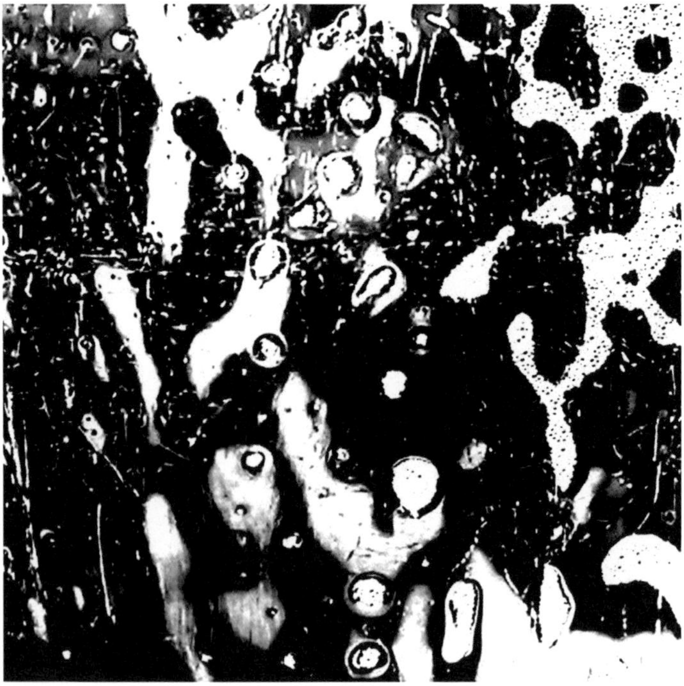

Sides of a glass of Jennings Cocker Hoop.
Haworth Old Hall Inn, Haworth. *WP*.

The Rise and Fall of the Butterfly

Golden Best

ptDoowerer... ptDoowerer... ptDoowerer...
Dive, Dive, Dive [181]
Woman teetering on a mountaintop
London's Burning, The Clash [182]
Tiles falling off the space shuttle [183]
P I N T
Broken shells on the strandline [184]
Hawksclough Bridge
Butterfly with wings detaching mid flight
Gatekeeper's House in the snow
Negative join the dots.

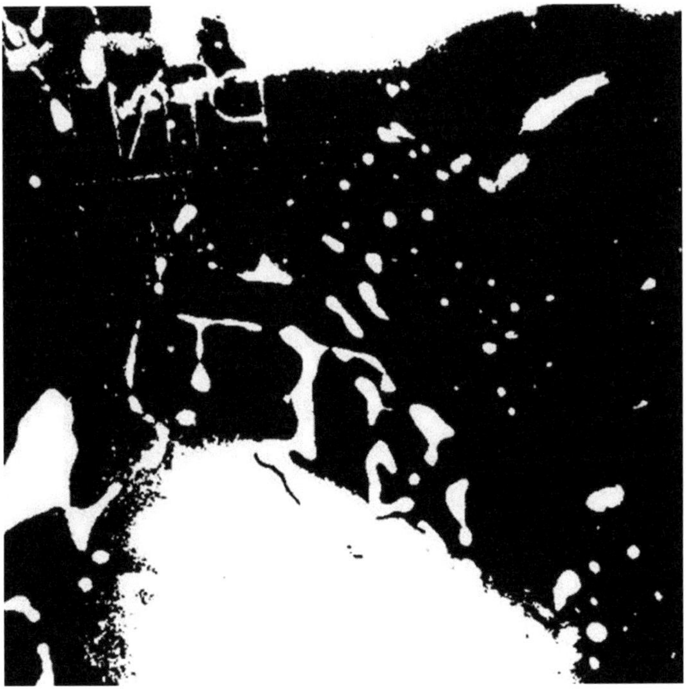

Sides of a glass of Timothy Taylor's Golden Best.
The Works, Sowerby Bridge. *JH.*

Broken Trust
Carlsberg

A female winking eye
Churn Milk Joan [185]
Raw cow's tongue
Geese flying west
Trust, front derailleur [186]
Skiers assembling at the top of a mountain
London Plane tree [187]
Engagement ring - broken
White noise television
K-9. [188]

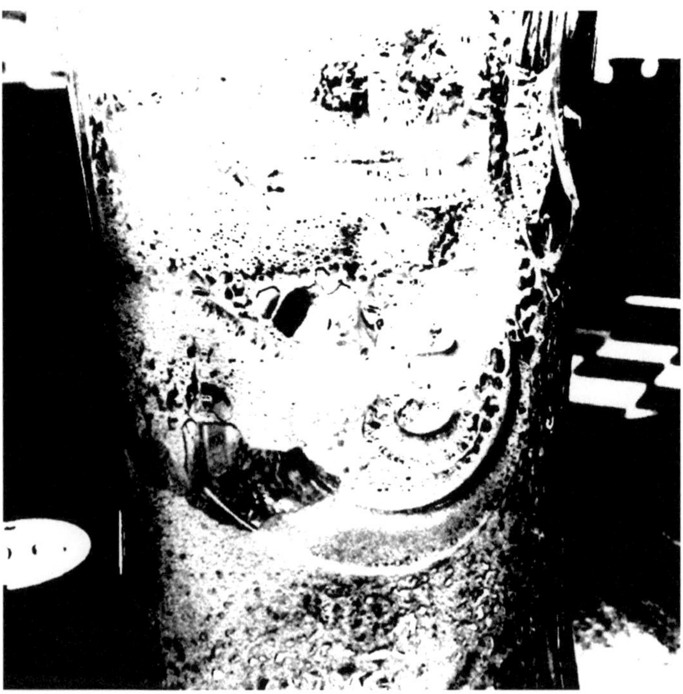

Sides of a branded pint glass of Carlsburg.
Table 106, The Standing Order, Derby. *WP.*

In a City Park

Bengali

Mother and daughter water sprites
diving down to a pearl

The world's oceans seen from space

A mole stuck in a drainpipe

Two badly made puppets fighting

A tree in a city park

Sperm approaching an egg

An exploding sun spot flume

An exploding carbonated drink

A seed germinating in the earth

Head of a sperm whale

Wile E. Coyote having just blown himself up. [189]

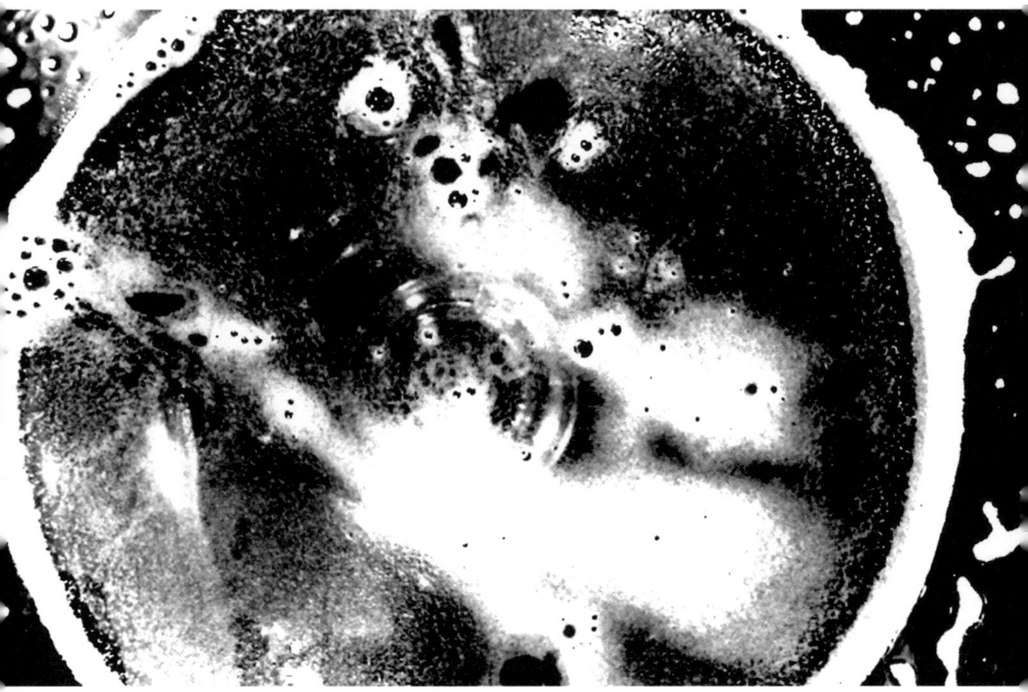

Surface of a glass of Sixpoint Craft Ales Bengali IPA.
Table 6, The Percy Shaw, Halifax. *JH.*

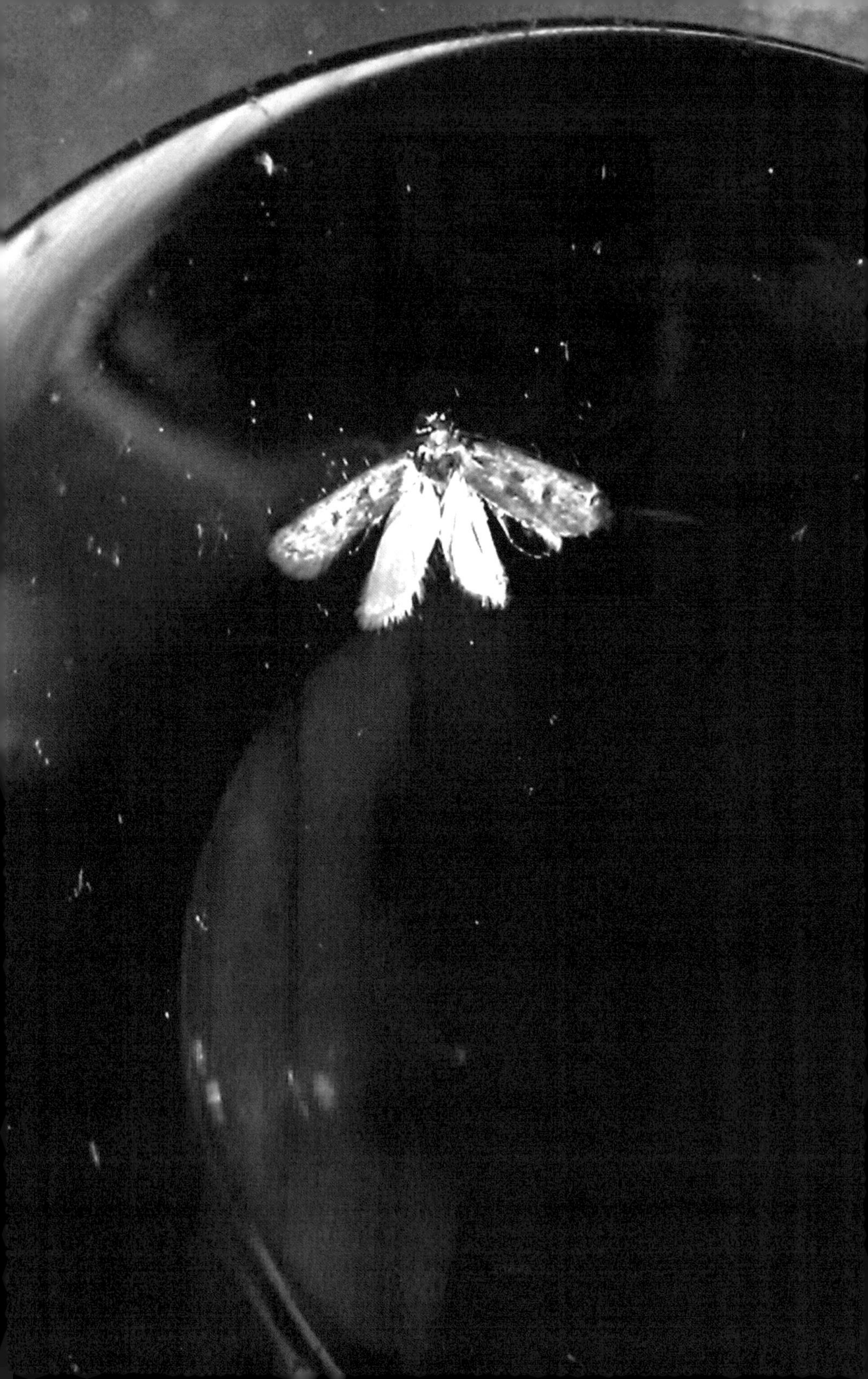

7 Sensory Miscellanea

of Oddly Shaped Treasures

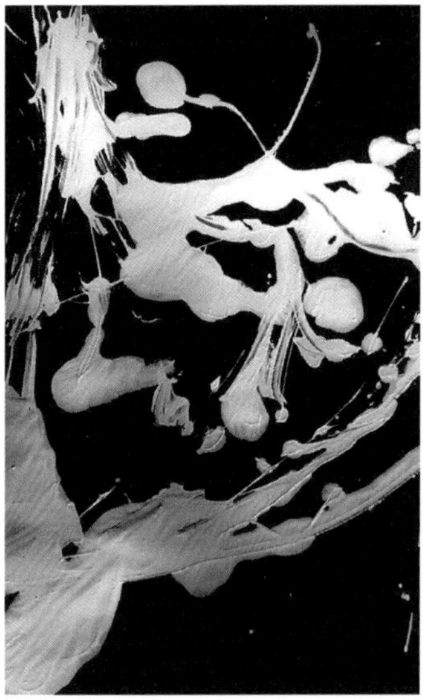

This section is a home for other liquid pareidolia happenings that are relatives of the rest of the poems in this book but too distant to comfortably stand beside them. A sort of charity shop of oddly shaped treasures just waiting for the right person to come along and buy them.

Feel free to browse without obligation …

A Perfect Square

A dancer doing a pirouette
A frog
A falling inverted heart
A dummy
CND symbol [190]
Chinese fishermen in traditional dress
A ram's head
Student's anatomical cutaway model of the brain
Australia
An old fashioned telephone
Plug on a chain
A wishbone from a chicken
A bell
An alien with an expanding head
Man in a wheel
One kidney
A lower case letter d
Five figures in a line
A parakeet
Logo of The Prince of Wales [191]
A net being cast
A clown laughing
Symbol of the artist formerly known as Prince [192]
A figure holding a knife, blade down, arm horizontal in front
Barbapapa [193]
A rolled up trouser leg
Pac-Man
The really annoying long eared
alien character from Star Wars [194]
A catfish face
A perfect square.

The composition of this piece predates all the poetry found in this book (except *Girl With The Wind in Her Hair* on page 29 which was written in 2013) and was in many ways a catalyst for the rest of the poems here. It is included therefore not only as a close relative to the main poems but to show the progression of the writer's practice.

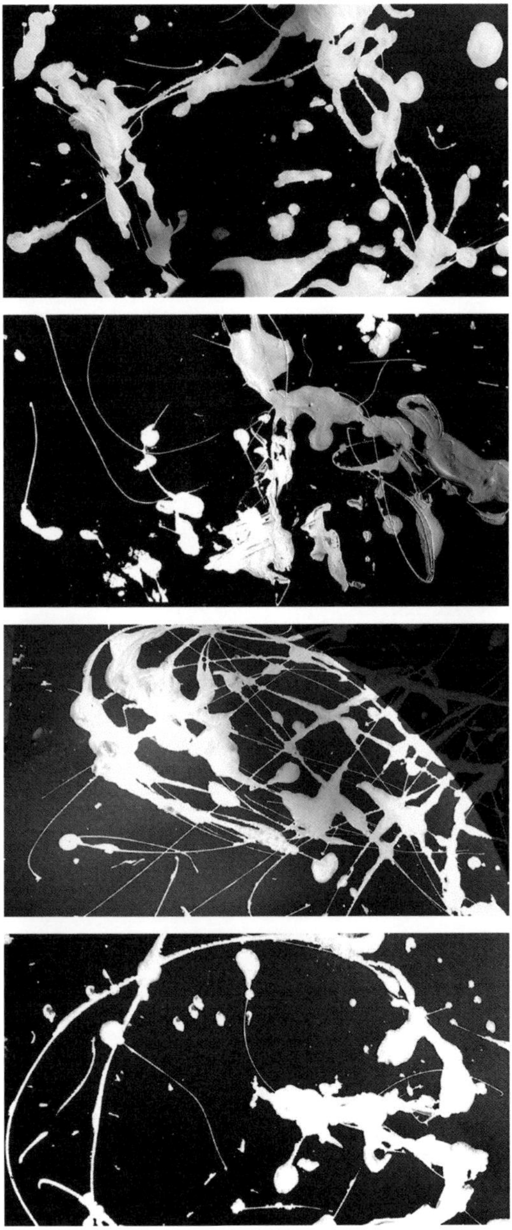

Above are paintings of four images out of the 30 observed in The English Channel at 4pm one day in April 2015.
Wake of the Dover to Calais ferry (*The Pride of Canterbury*).
Top to bottom: A perfect Square, A wishbone from a chicken, A net being cast, Pac-Man.

Few Could Endure that Terrible Gaze

Dr Pepper

An alien
A row of unnamed islands
The eye of Sauron [195]
Popper beads
Frogs eggs
Spider
Popcorn
A crab
Fish
Five dots equally spaced around a circle
then four in a perfect square
A whale shark [196]
A ram with horns
Tadpoles
The skin of The Thing [197]
England
A ring with a single diamond
A horseshoe
Australia
Avocado
Italy and Sicily
Mike Wazowski. [198]

Observations on and under the surface of a can of Dr Pepper after each pour into a white enamel mug and a small hungry caterpillar plastic cup.
In a van, Channel View Campsite, Brean, Somerset.

Jointly *composed with Maisy Howell*

Teenage Mutation

Glass of Water

1960's flying saucer
Teenage Mutant Ninja Turtle face [199]
A frog
A manta ray [200]
A cormorant drying its wings. [201]

Composed *from various comments harvested from shared Facebook postings*

Surface Tension
Côtes du Rhône

Snow Angel [202]
Floorboards awash with blood
Peach flesh
Figure waving wearing white trousers
Trying to sleep on a train at night
Traffic lights
Faint northern lights
A shocked face (on left fore-wing)
Small comet
Plum skin

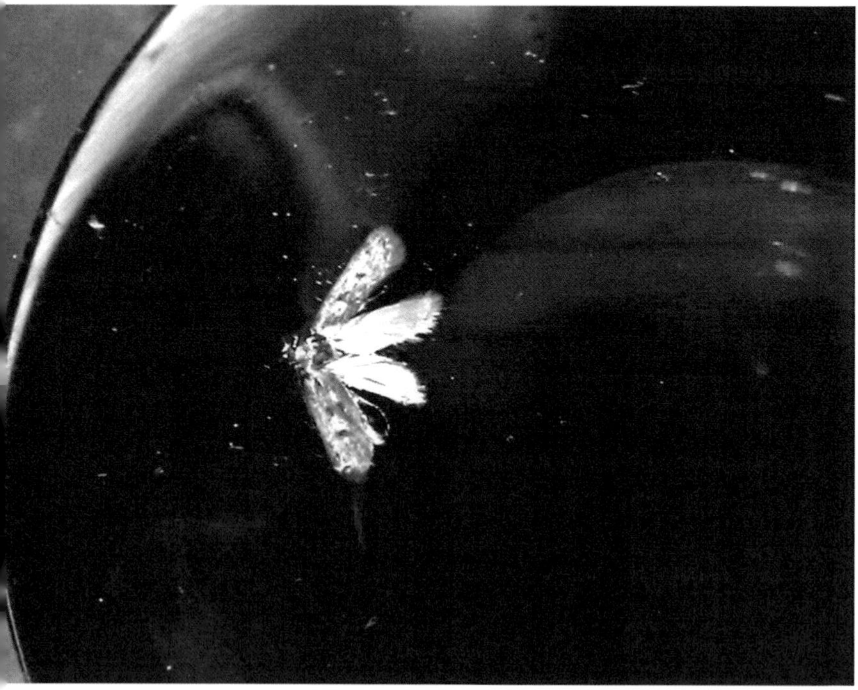

Stemless glass of Côtes du Rhône and its reflections. Included is a dead specimen of the Brown House-moth Hofmannophila pseudospretella. [204]

Reflections from a Torchlit Dream

Isle of Jura

Teapot handle
A lock of a lover's hair
Dyke sluice opening
Unknown space phenomenon
Ramsons caught in torchlight [203]
Waterslide
Shrouded figure
The start of a dream.

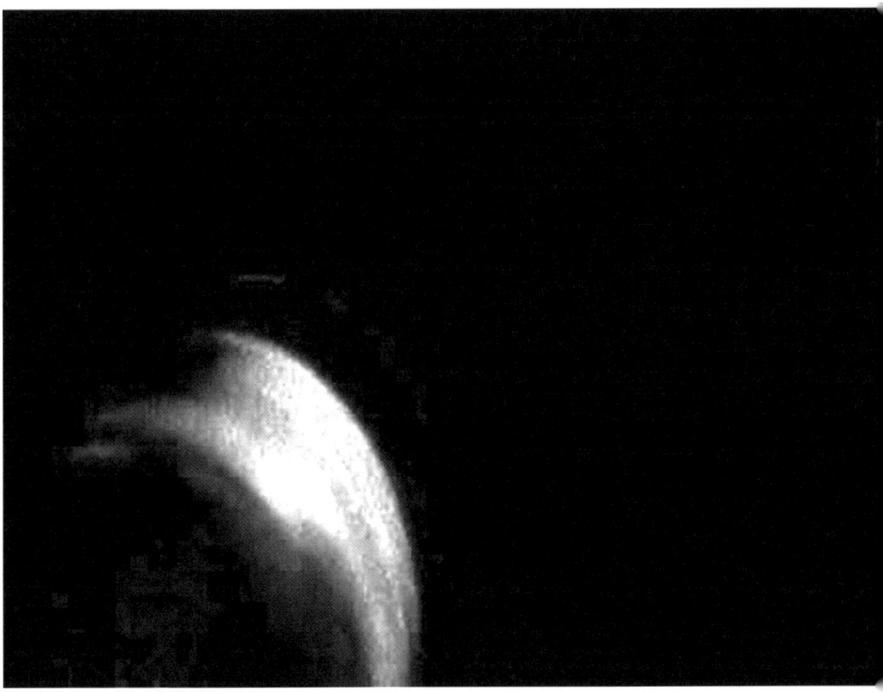

From a photograph through a glass of Isle of Jura single malt whisky.

Gift of Life
Oil Wheel

Stomach
Big toe
Tadpole with exceedingly long tail
Peas in pod
Whale swallowing a ball
Embryo developing
Smurf hat
Kangaroo throwing darts
Rain dripping off a blade of grass
Footprint
Pondweed
A 'giving' hand.

All images from a film of an oil wheel projection (6.14)

The Life of a Humpback Whale

A camel
A camel
Weasel
The back of a weasel
A whale
An extremely lifelike whale.

Adapted from a passage in Shakespeare's Hamlet
(Act 3, Scene 2). Text simplified and hybrid title added.

Jointly *composed with Hamlet and Polonius.*

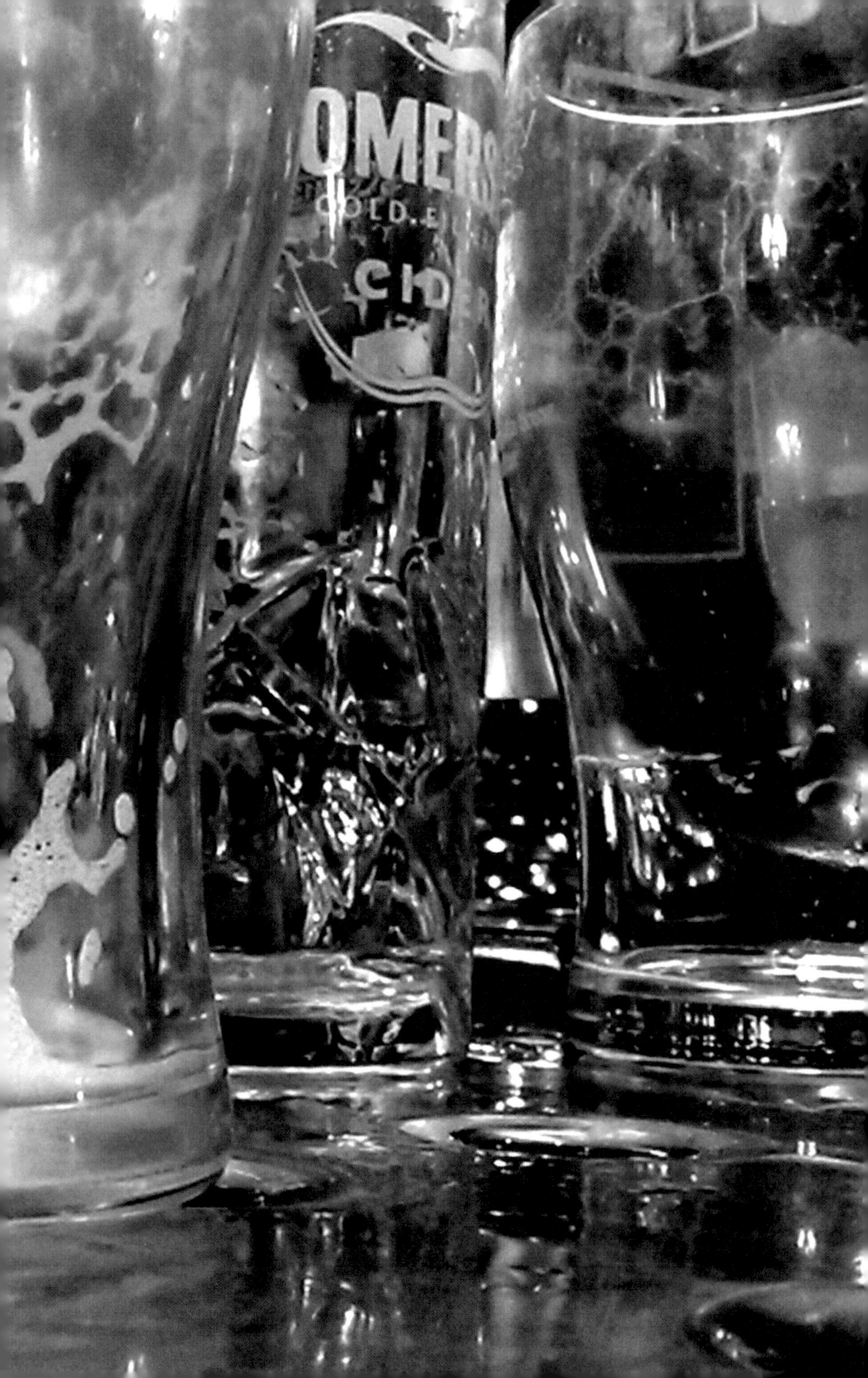
OMERS
OLD.E
CID

Appendices

Cabinet of Curiosities

For the surrealist artist who worshipped irrational juxtaposition, a cabinet of curiosities was a place where the bizarre could comfortably exist alongside the unexplained and ideas could emerge from the gaps in between.

Here, for the illumination of the reader I have listed some background detail and interesting facts relating to some of the more bizarre and unusual images conjured up in the process of compiling this book.

GLASS HALF FULL

1 Ayers Rock – A 350m high sandstone monolith known to the Aborigines as 'Uluru' and one of the most impressive natural landmarks in Australia. It is best observed during sunrise and sunset, when it often becomes transformed, taking on a violet/blue colour instead of its daytime terracotta.

2 Willy Wisp – A sprite and friend of Rupert the Bear. First appearing in the TV series *The Adventures of Rupert Bear* (1969 to 1977).

3 Batman – Comic book hero and caped crusader who fights crime with his sidekick Robin. Fist seen in DC comics in 1939 and since in many adaptations on TV and in film.

4 Indoor Boomerangs – Are usually made of foam and have three 'lobes' which enable them to be thrown safely indoors and return to their owner.

5 Kiwi – New Zealand bird of the family *Apteryx* not to be confused with the kiwi fruit or Chinese gooseberry. Kiwis are the smallest of the worlds flightless birds which also include ostriches, emus, rheas, and cassowaries, and are similar in size to a domestic chicken.

6 Ducks and Drakes – A game where flat stones are thrown horizontally, underarm so that they skim across the surface of water leaving rings of ripples as they 'skip'. The world record number of skips in a single throw is 51 by Russell 'Rock Bottom' Byars.

7 Sustrans Waymarker – Mileposts along numerous routes of the National Cycle Network, that take the form of an abstract tree, decorated with relief images illustrating the passage of time and evolution of life. Designed by John Mills to commemorate the millennium and developed by British charity Sustrans.

8 Oakley Sunglasses – One of the more expensive brands of sunglasses which have a distinctive shape. Often favoured by sportsmen.

9 Kateroo – A fictional creature, part Kangeroo and part cat.

10 Henri-Émile-Benoît Matisse – (1869-1954). A French artist, known for both his use of colour and his fluid and original draughtsmanship. Along with Pablo Picasso and Marcel Duchamp, Matisse is commonly regarded as one of the three artists who helped to define the revolutionary developments in the plastic arts in the opening decades of the 20th century and responsible for significant developments in painting and sculpture. *(Ref: e-Study Guide for: Contemporary Europe: A History* by James D. Wilkinson, 2013).

11 Pac-Man – A popular arcade game released in 1980, designed by Toru Iwatani.

12 Punch and Judy – Children's hand puppet entertainment performed by one puppeteer (or 'professor') in a booth and dating back to the 17th century. Traditionally the show follows a set plot involving outrageous violence between the characters of Pulcinella (Mr. Punch) his wife Judy, and other characters.

13 Flux Capacitor – In the 1985 film *Back to the Future*, Doctor Emmett Brown states that the flux capacitor "*is what makes time travel possible.*" He deployed such a device in his time travelling DeLorian car. In one scene, the car time-travelled to 04:29, on OCT 21 2015, a date celebrated by fans of the film. On this day no significant time-space anomalies were reported.

14 Gerard James Butler – Actor (born 1969).

15 Inspector Jacques Clouseau – A fictional character in Blake Edwards' farcical *The Pink Panther* series. Most popularly played by Peter Sellers.

16 Al Catpone – A dangerous feline gangster responsible for controlling the illegal milk trade during prohibition era Chicago. His ninth life was lost in a notorious gun battle.

17 Zig and Zag – Furry alien puppet twins from the planet Zog who became a popular feature on *The Big Breakfast*, Channel 4 TV, 1990's. The highlight of their singing career was *Them Girls Them Girls* which reached the top five in the UK singles charts.

18 The Ceiling Demons – (Founded 2011). An alternative Hip Hop band from Yorkshire whose members often wear black and white masks and hoodies.

19 Fred 'Freddy' Krueger – The main antagonist of the A Nightmare on Elm Street film series.

20 Menoptera – A race of creatures with features of bees from *Dr Who*, Season 2. *The Web Planet*. 1965.

21 Superlambanana – A sculpture in Liverpool by Japanese artist Taro Chiezo.

22 Curling Stones – Granite stones of approx. 40 pounds each used in the sport of curling in which teams of players slide stones on ice towards a circular target.

23 Ghetto Blaster – (Boombox or Brixton briefcase) A bulky cassette or CD player with two or more loudspeakers that can be carried by its handle.

24 Cashmere – A soft fibre used for weaving from the cashmere and other breeds of goat. Commonly classified as a type of wool but is in fact a type of hair.

25 Henry Spencer Moore – (1898 - 1986). An English sculptor and artist, best known for his semi-abstract large scale bronze sculptures of figures.

26 Solar Flare – A sudden release of magnetic energy from the sun's atmosphere. This phenomenon was first recorded in 1859 by Messrs Carrington and Hodgson.

27 The Traveler – A *Star Trek* character player by Eric Menyuk whose real name was unpronounceable by Humans. This mysterious humanoid had the ability to alter space, time and warp fields using only the power of his mind.

28 Chakras – In some Indian religions are considered to be the seven centres of spiritual power. They are often represented as a diagram of points on a vertical line running down the line of symmetry of the human body.

29 Rain Dance – The practice of performing a ritual dance to encourage rainfall is commonly associated with the First Nation tribes of North America, but the practice is also recorded in ancient China and Slavic countries.

30 Henge - An earthwork structure from the Neolithic period usually laid out in a circular format with a bank and ditch around the perimeter. Timber or stone circles and burial sites are sometimes found in the central flat area of the henge.

31 Cthulhu – A deity created by writer H.P. Lovecraft. The creature has since been featured in numerous popular culture references. Lovecraft depicts Cthulhu's anatomy as part man, dragon, and octopus.

32 Unicorn – A mythical beast taking the form of a white horse or goat with a single long tusk growing from its forehead. Unicorns are said to possess healing qualities and be able to purify poisonous water. In some versions of folklore they may only be captured by a virgin.

33 Scooby-Doo – A cartoon dog whose exploits have been broadcast on TV and in film since 1969. In the first series made by Hanna-Barbera productions the Great Dane accompanied his four teenage friends Fred, Velma, Daphne and Shaggy to solve supernatural mysteries in *Scooby-Doo, Where Are You!*

34 Mickey Mouse – One of the oldest animated cartoon characters, created in 1928 and the mascot of The Walt Disney Company. Before the 1940's Mickey's ears were animated to appear circular no matter which way he turned.

35 Elvis – Elvis Aaron Presley (1935-1977). Often called 'The King', Elvis was one of the most popular and significant singers and performers of his era. In 2005, Variety magazine placed him in the top ten of its '100 Icons of the Century', and The Discovery Channel put him in 8th place on its list of Greatest Americans.

36 The Cretan Bull – Greek mythology. The bull that Pasiphaë fell in love with, giving birth to the Minotaur.

37 Mr Blobby – An accident prone and chaotic character which featured on Noel Edmonds TV show, *Noel's House Party*, Although instantly memorable and popular for a time, the bulbous pink figure with yellow spots, and jiggling eyes was not well received critically.

38 Snoopy – The world-famous dog, also known as 'Joe Cool', is Charlie Brown's pet beagle in the comic strip *Peanuts*, created by cartoonist Charles Monroe Schulz. Snoopys first appearance was October 4, 1950.

39 Ecce homo (Translation: *Behold the man*) – The Latin words used by Pontius Pilate (*John 19:5*) when he presents a scourged Jesus Christ, bound and crowned with thorns, to a hostile crowd shortly before his Crucifixion.

40 Flamenco – Music and dance native to the Spanish regions of Andalusia, Extremadura and Murcia.

41 Gobi Desert – A large region in northern China and southern Mongolia bounded by the Altai mountains and steppes of Mongolia, the Tibetan Plateau and China. The word Gobi means 'desert' in Mongolian. Contrary to images often associated with a desert, much of the Gobi is not sandy but is covered with bare rock. Remarkably the temperature of the desert can vary up to 35 degree Centigrade within a 24 hour period.

42 Gypsy Tart – An extremely sweet pastry tart made with evaporated milk and muscovado sugar originating from The Isle of Sheppey in Kent and for many people a staple school dinner pudding.

43 The White House – The official residence of the President of the USA in Washington D.C. There are two lawns, North and South lawns which are used for official and informal gatherings. The Presidents helicopter also uses the South lawn as a landing area.

44 The Cow jumped over the moon – A line from the English nursery rhyme *'Hey Diddle Diddle'*, thought to date back to at least the 16th century. The interpretations of this and the other lines in the rhyme have been numerous but it may well be simply nonsense verse.

45 The Scream – The common name given to a collection of similar works by the expressionist artist Edvard Munch, painted between 1893 and 1910. One of the four versions was sold at Sotherby's for almost £80m in 2012.

46 Crunchie Bar – Originally introduced by J.S. Fry & Son in 1929 and later made by Cadbury, the Crunchie is a chocolate coated British confectionery with a honeycomb toffee centre.

47 Handlebar Moustache – As defined by the Handlebar Club who have met in London since 1947 is *'a hirsute appendage of the upper lip, with graspable extremities'*.

48 Spider Monkeys – Are large rainforest monkeys approximately two feet tall excluding the tail. They like to hang upside-down with all four limbs and the tail holding on to branches which gives them a spider-like appearance. They are also able to swing from branch to branch at a high speed.

49 Goat Wattles – A fleshy caruncles hanging from various parts of the head or neck in several groups of birds and mammals including goats. Sometimes called tassels in the case of a goat.

50 Whernside – A mountain in the Yorkshire Dales and one of the Yorkshire Three Peaks.

51 Brain Dots – A puzzle game for smart phones where a path is constructed between two balls in order to join them. When they touch another level is reached.

52 Berk – An egg-shaped blue creature from the British animated TV show, *The Trap Door* (1986). His common exclamations included "*Oh, Globbits!*" and "*Sniff that!*" which were always pronounced in a strong West Country accent.

53 Wind Cherub – Figures blowing wind were a popular addition to maps and charts as late as the 17th and 18th century. On some they appear as heads of old men, on others as Cherubs. (Ref: *The Story of Maps*, Lloyd Arnold Brown page 100).

54 Conga Eel – Comprising of a number of species, the life history of Conga Eels is still not fully understood. The Giant Conga can grow to over 7metres long.

55 Tintin et la Fusée Italienne – (Translation: *Tintin and the Italian Rocket*).

56 Pinocchio – A wooden puppet carved by Geppetto, that comes to life in the book *The Adventures of Pinocchio* (1883) by the Italian writer Carlo Collodi.

57 Amoebas – Single celled aquatic organisms having one or more nuclei surrounded by a flexible outer membrane.

58 Joan Miró – (1893-1983). A Spanish artist from Barcelona. He created celebrated work in a range of styles including tapestry, sculpture, ceramics and painting.

59 Ansel Easton Adams – (1902-1984). US photographer and environmentalist whose dramatic black-and-white landscapes of the American West, natably Yosemite National Park, are still widely reproduced, notably on calendars, posters, and in books.

60 Nora Batty – A fictional character from *Last of the Summer Wine* played by Kathy Staff between 1973 and 2008. The character became a national icon on the long running sitcom famous for wearing her pinny, wrinkled stockings and hair curlers.

61 Will-o'-the-Wisps – The not fully explained occurrence of ghostly lights seen by travellers especially in boggy or marshy areas. Also know by the names *Jack-o'-lantern* and *ignis fatuus* (foolish fire).

62 Conjoined Twins – The extremely rare occurrence of Identical twins that are joined in the mother's womb. The term 'Siamese' twins originates from the famous Siam born conjoined twins Chan and Eng Bunker (1811-1874) who became a feature of P.T. Barnum's Circus.

63 Twitchers – Committed bird-watchers who travel long distances to see a new species and add it to a species their 'lifelist', 'year list' etc.

64 Sandpiper – Shorebirds from the family *Scolopacidae.*

65 Oystercatcher – (*Haematopus ostralegusis*) a large, stocky, black and white wading bird with long, orange-red bill and reddish-pink legs.

66 The Elephant Man – Joseph Merrick (1862-90) became disfigured due to large tumours growing on his body. In 1884 he found an ally in a Leicester music hall owner Sam Torr, and together they conceived the successful act of *The Elephant Man* where Merrick would display his increasingly misshapen body. The audience were told that Merrick's appearance was due to his mother being frightened by an elephant during pregnancy..

67 Ewoks – Small hunter-gatherer teddy bear like bipeds appearing in the Star Wars films. Their home planet is the forest moon of Endor.

68 SpongeBob SquarePants – The lead character in an American animated television series created by marine biologist and animator Stephen Hillenburg for Nickelodeon.

69 The Simpsons – An American animated television series featuring the fictional characters: ***Charles Montgomery Plantagenet Shicklgruber Burns.*** Also known as Monty Burns and Mr. Burns, he is the owner and manager of the Springfield Nuclear Power Plant and the main antagonist in the show. ***Bartholomew JoJo 'Bart' Simpson*** is part of the Simpson family. He is voiced by Nancy Cartwright and first appeared on television in The Tracey Ullman Show *Good Night* on April 19, 1987. Cartoonist Matt Groening created and designed Bart while waiting in the lobby of James L. Brooks' office.

70 The Mercator Projection – A cylindrical map projection devised by the Flemish cartographer Gerardus Mercator in 1569 which became a standard for nautical navigation.

71 Endor – (Aka: *The Forest Moon of Endor*). A small moon orbiting the planet Endor covered with forests of giant trees. This enchanted world is the native native home of the Ewoks (see note 64) in the Star Wars universe.

72 Stormtroopers – Feature widely in George Lucas' epic space opera *Star Wars*. They are the elite soldiers of the Galactic Empire keeping thousands of star systems throughout the galaxy in line. They became major symbols of authority.

73 Idents – The animations shown by a television channel between programs or during continuity announcements. The spinning globe was used by the BBC from 1969 to 1974.

74 Wookiee(s) – A fictional intelligent species of tall hair covered bipeds from the planet Kashyyyk. The most notable Wookiee being Chewbacca who was Han Solo's companion in the Star Wars universe.

75 Skellybob – Urban slang for skeleton.

76 The Loch Ness Monster or 'Nessie' – An alleged plesiosaur-like creature living in Loch Ness, a long deep lake near Inverness, Scotland. Many sightings of the 'monster' have been recorded, dating back to St. Columba, an Irish monk from the 6th century, who some believe confronted and tamed the 'water-beast'.

77 Stag Beetles (Family: *Lucanidae*) – So called due to the large and distinctive mandibles found on the males, which resemble the antlers of stags. *Lucanus cervus* is the largest terrestrial insect in Europe.

78 Honshu – The largest and most populous island of Japan. The nation's main island and the seventh largest island in the world.

79 Roobarb – Now a cult animated BBC TV series of thirty four minute long episodes written by Grange Calveley, narrated by Richard Briers and animated by Bob Godfrey The theme is that of a friendly rivalry between Roobarb the green dog and Custard the pink cat from next door. First shown in 1974.

80 Ibex – A wild mountain goat with long, thick ridged horns and a beard, found in parts of central Asia and in Ethiopia.

81 Hiroshima – Founded in 1589, Hiroshima is the largest city in the Chūgoku region of western Honshu (see 78) and the first city in the world to suffer a strike by a nuclear weapon during WWII, 6 Aug 1945.

82 Bernard John Manning – (1930-2007). A controversial Mancunian, comedian and nightclub owner, specialising in the telling of irreverent jokes targeting people from all walks of life including ethnic minority groups, which led to frequent criticism of Manning's act and accusations that it was racist.

83 Slimer – A ghost from the *Ghostbusters* films made of pure Ectoplasm and the first ghost successfully captured. He is well known for his gigantic appetite and the slime he leaves behind when he passes through solid objects.

84 Alex Brooker – (Born 1984). An English journalist and presenter, best known for his television work with Channel 4.

85 Peppa Pig – Main character of the early years animated TV series of the same name, first aired in 2004. She enjoys dressing up, going to playgroup and jumping in puddles. Her father, Daddy Pig is an Architect.

PARK LIFE

86 Milky Way – The galaxy containing our own Solar System. In areas of low light pollution the Milky Way can be seen as a faintly glowing band of 'milky' light spanning the night sky.

87 Bibendum – Commonly referred to as the Michelin Man, is the symbol of the Michelin tire company. Introduced at the Lyon Exhibition of 1894 where the Michelin brothers had a stand.

88 Baily's Beads – Beads of light caused by sunlight still being able to reach the Earth through lunar valleys shortly before a total eclipse of the sun.

89 Anticyclone – A large scale meteorological effect where winds circulate around a central low pressure.

90 Cul-de-sac – French, meaning 'bottom of the sack'. Origin 1730-40.

91 Super Mario – A popular series of platform video games which first appeared in 1985. Created by Nintendo featuring their mascot, Mario. Mushroom power-ups appear in almost every version of the game.

92 BrewDog – A Scottish brewery in Ellon, Aberdeenshire founded in 2007.

93 Constellation of Orion – Named after the hunter featured in Greek mythology. It is one of the most conspicuous constellations in the night sky. Its brightest stars are Rigel and Betelgeuse.

94 Sideburns – (Sideboards or side whiskers). Facial hair extending from the hairline down each side of a man's face in front of and to below the ears. The style is named after American Civil War general Ambrose Burnside who was famous for an exaggerated form of this facial hairstyle.

95 Halva – (Sanskrit: Meaning '*a mixture*'). The confectioner/baker is called a 'Halwai'. It refers to a broad range of dense, sweet confectionery made from a variety of ingredients across the world.

96 The Ant Hill Mob – A group of 1920s gangsters who competed in the TV cartoon program, *Wacky Races*. They drove in car number 7, The Bullet-proof Bomb (also known as The Roaring Plenty).

97 Buttress – An architectural structure usually made of stone or brick used to strengthen or support a wall. Either built into the original design or added afterwards.

98 Hurricane Katia – An intense and prolonged tropical cyclone that caused minor damage and disruption throughout the Lesser Antilles and European regions including the UK during September 2011.

99 Epsilon – The fifth letter of the Greek alphabet ('*E*').

100 Bat-signal – A searchlight on the roof of the Gotham Police Department that projected the image of a bat onto the clouds, and used to summon Batman for help when necessary.

101 Cyber Mice – An online game where mice have to be shepherded to a piece of cheese within a time limit using barriers made from matchsticks, coins and other items.

102 Rheumatism Bracelet – Although scientifically unproven, the wearing of copper and magnetic bracelets to combat rheumatism has been popular since the 1970s, a belief that can be traced back 2000 years.

103 Propeller appearing to rotate backwards – This stroboscopic effect is a visual phenomenon occurring when the view of a rotating object is represented by a series of short samples as distinct from a continuous view also termed the 'wagon-wheel effect'.

104 Stratus – Flat, hazy, featureless clouds of low altitude varying in color from dark gray to nearly white. (Ref: *The World Meteorological Organisation International Cloud Atlas*, Volume 1. 1975).

105 The Pequod – A fictitious 19th century Nantucket whaling ship that appears in the 1851 novel *Moby-Dick* by American author Herman Melville.

106 Wilma Flintstone (née *Pebble*) – A character in the TV animated series *The Flintstones*. Wilma is Strong-willed but level-headed, wife of Fred Flintstone and mother of Pebbles. Her personality was based on that of Alice Kramden, wife of Ralph Kramden from the 1950s TV series *The Honeymooners*.

THE GREEN ROOM

107 The Thought Fox – One of the most celebrated and anthologised poems of Poet Laureate, Ted Hughes appearing in his first collection of poems, *The Hawk in the Rain* (1957).

108 Chocolate Kisses – A brand of confectionary made by the American Hershey company having the distinctive shape of a flat-bottomed teardrop.

109 Froglets – A trio of small frog-like aliens with large eyes, orange bodies and black stalk-like legs, who travel through space in a top hat. They feature in some episodes of the cult animated TV series, *The Clangers*, originally made by Smallfilms and broadcast in 1969. (See 150).

110 The Great Bear – A constellation in the northern hemisphere, also known as *Ursa Major.* Its most recognizable group of seven relatively bright stars are commonly known as *The Big Dipper, The Wagon* or *The Plough*, used as a navigational pointer towards the pole star, Polaris in *Ursa Minor.*

111 The Witch-king of Angmar – Also know as the Lord of the Nazgûl or the Black Captain. A major character in J.R.R. Tolkien's world of Middle-earth in the novel *The Lord of the Rings.* He is the chief of the Nazgûl (Ringwraiths), servants of the Dark Lord Sauron.

112 Mount Rushmore National Memorial – An enormous sculpture carved into a granite cliff face near Keystone, South Dakota, in the USA. Sculpted between 1934 and 1939 by Gutzon Borglum and his son Lincoln, it features 20 metre high likenesses of the heads of four presidents, Washington, Jefferson, Roosevelt and Lincoln.

113 Spiv – A name sometimes given to a shady character who may try to sell counterfeit objects at a discounted price, e.g., the character of Private Joe Walker played by James Beck in The TV series *Dads Army.*

114 Gerald Anthony Scarfe – (Born 1936). An English artist. He has worked as editorial cartoonist for *The Sunday Times* and illustrator for *The New Yorker.*

JAVA LOUNGE

115 Mount Everest – The Highest mountain summit in the world at nearly 9,000 meters above sea level. Called *Chomolungma* in Tibet and *Sagarmatha* in Nepal it lies in the Mahalangur section of the Himalayan mountain range.

116 The Grimm Fairytales – A total of 170 stories published by Jacob and Wilhelm Grimm between 1812 and 1822 including *Snow White, Cinderella* and *Hansel and Gretel.* The early volumes were much criticized and by many were not regarded as being suitable for children.

117 Spiral Arm Galaxy – One of the basic shapes of galaxies. Gigantic arrays of individual stars linked by the forces of gravity with arms of stars reaching out tens of thousands of light years.

118 Chinese Dragon – Dragons have been associated with Chinese culture since neolithic times. It is seen as a symbol of power, strength and good fortune. A dragon featured on the flag of China until 1912.

119 The Curious Incident of the Dog in the Night-time – Originally A phrase used as part of an explanation of the methods of deductive reasoning by Sherlock Holmes and part of the dialog between himself and Inspector Gregory of Scotland Yard in *The Adventure of Silver Blaze.*

120 The Adventure of the Dancing Men – One of the short stories from the collection '*The Return of Sherlock Holmes*' by British author Sir Arthur Conan Doyle, who ranked this particular tale third in his list of favourites. It features Mr. Hilton Cubitt of Ridling Thorpe Manor in Norfolk who finds mysterious stick figures chalked on his property. Trouble is not far behind for him and his wife Elsie.

121 Saint Bernard – A dog breed, originally used to guard the grounds of Switzerland's Great Saint Bernard Hospice, as well as to help find and save lost and injured alpine travellers.

122 Lunar Lander – Or Apollo Lunar Module (originally the Lunar Excursion Module) successfully transported American astronauts on the final stage of their mission to the moons surface.

123 David Michael Hasselhoff – (Born 1952). Nicknamed 'The Hoff' is an American actor, singer, producer, and businessman. Famous for his leading role as Michael Knight on *Knight Rider* and as L.A. County Lifeguard Mitch Buchannon in the series *Baywatch.*

124 U-boat – An anglicised shortening of the German, *Unterseeboot* (undersea boat) deployed by the German navy to primarily target merchant convoys and thereby disable vital trade routes.

125 Vinyl Record – A continuous spiral groove of information, transferred from a copper plate onto a circular vinyl disc when pressed together. It is then listened to on a record player that spins at speeds of 331/3 or 45 RPM (Revolutions Per Minute), that has a diamond cutting stylus mounted in a head, which vibrates inside the groove to create audio playback.

126 Water Boatman - *Corixa punctata*, is a common water insect. It has long hind legs, covered in hairs, that are used like paddles to swim. Its front legs are very short and are used to scoop up food. Males attract females with a 'courtship song', produced by rubbing their front legs against a ridge on their head.

127 Slime Mold - (Many-headed slime, *Physarum polycephalum*). The habitat of slime molds are moist and cool shaded areas such as woodland where they can be found on decaying leaves and dead logs. Under laboratory study the mould has shown 'intelligent' characteristics similar to those observed in single-celled creatures.

128 Peloton d'exécution - (French. Trans: *Firing Squad*). Used by soldiers to describe an execution or to ceremonially discharge weapons.

129 Argyle Socks - The Scottish argyle pattern is usually composed of diamond shapes with overlayed diagonal lines and is derived from the Clan Campbell tartan of Western Scotland. It is also associated with the patterned socks of the Scottish Highlanders since around the 17th century.

BEER IS GOOD

130 Noddy - A wooden character wearing a tall hat with a bell, who drives a yellow car with large red mudguards, created by English author Enid Blyton. Initially published in print between 1949 and 1963 Blyton's creations went on to be adapted for TV to make Noddy and his Toyland friends a household name.

131 Seventh Wave - A common belief has entered popular culture through music and literature that out of a certain number of waves every seventh wave will be much larger than the rest.

132 Jalapeño Pepper - (Pronounced: *hala-pee-no*). Members of the capsicum family which can vary in heat from moderate to very hot. They are approximately 4cm long and ripen from green to scarlet red and are rated at 3,500 to 10,000 Scoville heat units in comparison to the scotch bonnet pepper which can reach 350,000 units. Chipotle peppers are Jalapeños that have been dried and smoked.

133 Snow Cornice - From the Italian *cornice* meaning 'ledge'. An overhanging edge of snow on a ridge or the crest of a mountain.

134 Pinball - An arcade game comprising a table like glass topped cabinet in which steel balls are manipulated by flippers. Points are scored by the balls striking targets. The aim of the game is to score as many points or keep the balls in play for as long as possible. The game featured in the 1969 rock opera album *Tommy* by English band, *The Who*.

135 Calabash - A style of curved pipe made famous in theatre, film and TV representations of the detective Sherlock Holmes.

136 Transporter - A fictional teleportation machine used in the Star Trek universe. Transporters convert a person or object into an energy pattern (dematerialisation), then 'beam' it to a target, where it is reconverted into matter (rematerialisation).

137 Holstein Friesians (Abbr. *Friesians* in Europe, *Holsteins* in North America) - A breed of cattle known today as the world's highest-production dairy animals.

138 Moon Buggy - The Lunar Roving Vehicle (LRV) or moon buggy featured in the 1971 film *Diamonds Are Forever*, where it is stolen by Bond as he escapes a laboratory. There are three LRVs still on the Moon from the Apollo space program.

139 Nebulae - Singular *nebula* (Latin for *cloud*) is a vast interstellar formation of dust, helium, hydrogen, and other gases.

140 Swarf - Pieces of metal, wood, or plastic that are the debris or waste resulting from machining, woodworking etc.

141 Uffington White Horse - A 100m long prehistoric horse design which features on a hillside near Wantage, Oxfordshire. The design is created in deep trenches filled with crushed white chalk.

142 Spider-Man - A Superhero character created by Marvel Comics writer-editor Stan Lee and writer-artist Steve Ditko in 1962. He acquired his super strength and other powers after being bitten by a radioactive spider.

143 The Watcher in the Water - A mysterious and horrifying octopus like beast which lives in the pool outside the Westgate of Moria in Tolkien's Middle-earth legendarium. It appears in *The Fellowship of the Ring* where it attacks the group of travellers.

144 The Old Grey Whistle Test - An influential BBC music show of the 1970s and 80s presented by Bob Harris and others. Although not the original titles, the opening sequence of the animated kicking male figure made up of stars, became synonymous with the show.

145 The Croctopus - A fictional beast. Half crocodile, half octopus (or squid). It will not be found in any known reference books.

146 Baileys Irish Cream – An Irish whiskey and cream based liqueur, made by Gilbeys of Ireland.

147 Beret – A soft, usually felt or knitted cap with a flat top and optional pom-pom. Archeology has revealed that hats similar to the modern beret existed as long ago as the Bronze Age in Northern Europe. Famous beret wearers include Thelonius Monk, Frank Spencer, Pablo Picasso and Che Guevara.

148 Pitcher Plant – A carnivorous plant that has evolved modified leaves known as pitfall traps, a prey-trapping mechanism featuring a deep cavity or pitcher filled with liquid.

149 Cookie Monster – A blue hairy googly eyed Muppet from the children's TV show, *Sesame Street.* Well known for his insatiable appetite and famous eating phrases such as "*Me want cookie*!" "*Me eat cookie!*" and "*Om nom nom nom*".

150 Clangers – A children's TV series created by Smallfilms (Oliver Postgate and Peter Firmin). First broadcast in 1969 it features a family of moon dwelling mouse-like creatures who communicate in whistles. They share their planetoid with a Soup Dragon, Sky Moos, Iron Chicken, and Froglets, amongst other strange beings (See 109).

151 Hopeful Monsters – An album by the Manchester based band The Cygnet Ring. Format: Cassette. Released: 1992 (North South). Band Members: Rus Harrison - Vocals, Guitar, Stephen Broomhead - Vocals, Electric guitar, Geoff Donkin - Drums, Geoff Ralph - Bass.

152 BASE Jumping – The adrenaline sport of leaping from a cliff or man made structure and parachuting to the ground. B.A.S.E is an acronym that stands for building, antenna, span, and Earth, four categories of fixed objects a base jumper can utilise.

153 North Face of the Eiger – A hidden door concealing a shaft which once enabled workmen to dispose of rubble during the construction of a railway tunnel within the mountain. More than once it has offered an escape route to mountaineers who have found themselves in difficulties.

154 Verdigris – The common name for the natural green patina formed when copper is weathered and exposed to air over a period of time. It used to be a common pigment in paints.

MONOCHROME ALTERNATIONS

155 Frankenstein – A novel written by Mary Shelley in which the science student Victor Frankenstein creates a grotesque creature in a scientific experiment. First published anonymously in 1818.

156 Cascade – The commonest juggling pattern with odd numbers of objects where throws alternate in an arc, hand to hand.

157 Beelzeboul – Greek spelling of dried cuttlefish from Crete.

158 Pop Art – A British art movement emerging in the mid 1950s. It presented a challenge to the traditions of fine art by including imagery from popular culture such as advertising material and news.

159 The Master and Margarita – A novel by Soviet author Mikhail Bulgakov, published in 1967 but written some 30 years earlier. It is considered by many to be one of the greatest novels of the 20th century.

160 Zygons – A fictional extraterrestrial race first featured on the popular TV series, *Dr Who* in 1975. Zygons rely on their ability to shape-shift in order to conceal themselves amongst earth's human population. When fleeing the destruction of their home planet Zygor, one of their organic spacecraft crash landed in Loch Ness where they used a Skarasen as their ally, (known to humans as the Loch Ness Monster. (See 76).

161 The Carnival of the Animals – An orchestral score in 14 parts written in 1886 by the French composer Camille Saint-Saëns (1835-1921). The piece was first performed shortly after his death in 1922 and has since become one of the composer's best known works.

162 The Saltwater Crocodile (*Crocodylus porosus*) – is the largest of all living reptiles. Also known as the Indo-Pacific crocodile or sea-going crocodile. Thankfully its habitat does not include the coastline of the United Kingdom.

163 Old Mother Shipton – Ursula Southeil (1488–1561) was born in a cave in the Yorkshire town of Knaresborough, now a tourist attraction known as Mother Shipton's Cave. She was said to be a soothsayer and prophetess and it is believed she foretold of the Great Fire of London.

164 David Hockney's 'Splash' – 1966-7. These three paintings depict a splash in a Californian swimming pool.

165 Archerfish (*Toxotidae*) – Are known for their habit of preying on land-based insects and other small animals by shooting them down with water droplets from their specialised mouths.

166 Moby Dick - A seafaring novel written by Herman Melville in 1851 in which an obsessed captain Ahab hunts down Moby Dick the white whale, in his vessel, the Pequod. The novel was not successful during the life of the author but is now regarded as an outstanding work of Romanticism and one of the greatest tales of the sea ever written. (See 105).

167 William Heath Robinson - (1872-1944). An English cartoonist and illustrator best known for drawings of ridiculously complicated machines for achieving simple objectives.

168 Lee-Enfield Rifle - One of the most successful bolt-action rifles ever produced. First manufactured in 1895 it is estimated that some 17 million weapons have been made.

169 Scrimshaw - Carvings and engravings in bone or ivory, specifically made by sailors and whalers.

170 Land of Nod - Slang for 'sleep'.

171 Oil Wheel Projection - The psychedelic 1960's lighting effect of merging and evolving colours and patterns. Where a rotating sealed wheel of dye and glycerine is placed in a projector.

172 Aborigine - A person indigenous to the Australian continent.

173 The Perseids - A prolific meteor shower associated with the comet Swift–Tuttle. So called because the point from which they appear to come, called the radiant, lies in the constellation Perseus.

174 Wilson, Keppel and Betty - A British music hall act popular in the 1950's. The 'sand dance', performed by the lithe and lanky Wilson and Keppel, demonstrated synchronised and comedic gestures which parodied the postures of Egyptian tomb art figues, while Betty looked on. During the life of the act there were at least eight different Bettys.

175 Shower Scene - *Psycho* (1960). American psychological thriller-horror film directed by Alfred Hitchcock. The films pivotal and most famous scene involves the murder of Marion Crane in the shower and has become one of the best known in cinema. This one scene alone took seven days and involved 78 camera different angles.

176 Pennies from Heaven - Was popularised by the film *Pennies from Heaven* (1936) and in particular by the Oscar-nominated hit song of the same name written by Burke and Johnston and sung by Bing Crosby. It has since become a crooner's standard and featured in the repertoires of the likes of Frank Sinatra.

177 Romanesque - Pertaining to the artistic style which prevailed during the Roman Empire.

178 Gitanes (Translation: *Gypsy women*) - A French brand of cigarettes sold in many varieties produced by Imperial Tobacco. The traditional packaging depicts a Spanish gypsy woman in silhouette playing the tambourine wreathed in smoke.

179 Jalebi - A sweet popular in countries of South Asia, the Middle East, North and East Africa. It is made by deep frying maida flour batter in pretzel or circular shapes, which are then soaked in sugar syrup.

180 Lichens - Composite organisms comprising both a fungus and an alga. (Algae being very simple plants). The two organisms form such a close partnership that they seem to be a single individual entirely different in appearance to either of the two constituent parts. There are more than 1,700 species of lichen in the UK.

181 'ptDoowerer' - An attempt to represent in letters the sound made by a submarine's echo sounding pings.

182 London's Burning - A song by English punk rock band, *The Clash* from their debut album released in 1977.

183 Tiles - Used on the space shuttle to shield it from the heat of re-entry were prone to falling off. Their attachment was a slow manual operation (nearly two man-years of work for every flight). Made slower by the glue drying so fast that a new batch needed mixing every couple of tiles. To speed up the process the technicians spat in the glue so it took longer to harden. However this weakened the adhesive bond between the tiles and the shuttle's aluminium shell.

184 Strandline - A mark left behind on the beach after high tide, typically composing of debris such as seawead and pebbles.

185 Churn Milk Joan - A solitary carved gritstone monument 2.1m in height. The feature is post-medieval in date but reuses stone bearing prehistoric cup and ring markings. Situated on Midgley Moor, Calderdale. *Grid Ref.* SE 01978 27685

186 Derailleur - A variable-ratio, chain driven transmission system used on bicycles where the chain is derailed as it moves between sprockets. From the French word describing a train derailed from its tracks.

187 London Plane (planetree, or hybrid plane) – A deciduous tree of the Platanus genus noted for its ability to adapt to urban conditions and its resistance to pollution. The tree can grow to a height of 20-30 meters, has large maple like leaves and exfoliating bark.

188 K-9 (retroactively K-9 Mark I) – A robot dog and companion of the fourth doctor in the *Dr Who* TV series played by Tom Baker. Initially appearing in *The Invisible Enemy* (1977) as the creation of Professor Marius in the year 5000.

189 Wile E. Coyote – 'Coyote' was the rival of *The Road Runner,* a fast moving ground bird whom he repeatedly attempts and fails to capture. Created by animator Chuck Jones for Warner Bros. *Looney Tunes* and *Merrie Melodies* series of cartoons, first broadcast in 1949. Jones based the character on the description of a coyote in Mark Twain's book '*Roughing It*'.

SENSORY MISCELLANEA

190 CND – The Campaign for Nuclear Disarmament formed in the UK in 1957 with the aim of campaigning for UK and global nuclear disarmament.

191 Logo of the Prince of Wales – Prince Charles is strongly associated with his personal insignia, *The Prince of Wales's Feathers*, a heraldic badge comprising a gold coronet encircling three white ostrich feathers. A dark blue ribbon below bears the motto *'Ich Dien'* (Trans: *I serve*).

192 The Artist Formerly Known as Prince – Musician Prince's name became a strange symbol he called 'the love symbol.' As such he no longer went by the name 'Prince' and insisted on being referred to as 'The Artist Formerly Known as Prince.'

193 Barbapapa – (From *barbe à papa* or *Daddy's beard*, French for 'candy floss'). The title of a series of childrens books originally in French and generic name for a family of shape changing characters. Written by Annette Tison and Talus Taylor in the 1970's, the books were translated into over 30 languages and also adapted into cartoons.

194 Jar Jar Binks – A character from the *Star Wars* series of films. Being a Gungan, Binks was lanky and spoke with a unique accent using simple expressions, a characteristic which many critics of the film found irritating. Despite being naïve and clumsy, he contributed greatly to the Galactic Republic, both for good and ill. George Lucas once stated that he had based the character on Disney's cartoon dog, *Goofy.*

195 Eye of Sauron – Featured in *The Lord of the Rings*, the Eye of Sauron was a symbol adopted by the Dark Lord during the Second and Third Age. It was said that few could endure the eye's terrible gaze.

196 Whale Shark (*Rhincodon typus*) – The largest fish in the world which can measure up to 12 meters in length.

197 The Thing (Benjamin 'Ben' Grimm) – A Marvel Comics superhero. As a member of the Fantastic Four, Grimm's skin became a thick craggy covering of large orange rocky plates following his exposure to cosmic rays.

198 Michael 'Mike' Wazowski – A monster character voiced by Billy Crystal in the films *Monsters Inc.,* and *Monsters University* made by Pixar. He has a green ball-shaped body, a single big eyeball and two small horns.

199 The Teenage Mutant Ninja Turtles (or Ninja Turtles) – Leonardo, Michelangelo, Raphael and Donatello are four fictional turtles who utilise their martial arts training to defeat evil whilst remaining hidden from society. Originally a comic strip in the 1980's the adventures of this popular reptilian quartet were later adapted for TV and film.

200 Manta Ray (*M. birostris* and *M. alfredi*) – Large ocean dwelling rays up to seven meters in width these ocean dwelling fish derive their name from the Spanish, 'Manta' meaning mantle (cloak or blanket) and are also sometimes called 'devil fish' due to their horns.

201 Cormorant (*Phalacrocorax carbo*) – A large black, prehistoric looking waterbird with a long neck relatively common in the UK. These birds are master fishermen and traditionally, in the East, were trained to aid humans catch fish.

202 Snow Angel – A design made in fresh snow by lying on one's back and moving one's arms up and down, and one's legs from side to side, to form the shape of an angel. Making snow angels is a common childhood game.

203 Ramsons (*Allium ursinum*) – Commonly known as wild garlic, is a wild relative of chives. The leaves, buld and flowers can be used in cooking. It's latin name is due to the brown bear's fondness of the plant.

204 Brown House-moth (*Hofmannophila pseudospretella)* – A common inhabitant of houses, this species is found throughout the British Isles, often on indoor walls as it begins to get dark. It is an Asian species introduced into Europe and many other parts of the world in the 1840s.

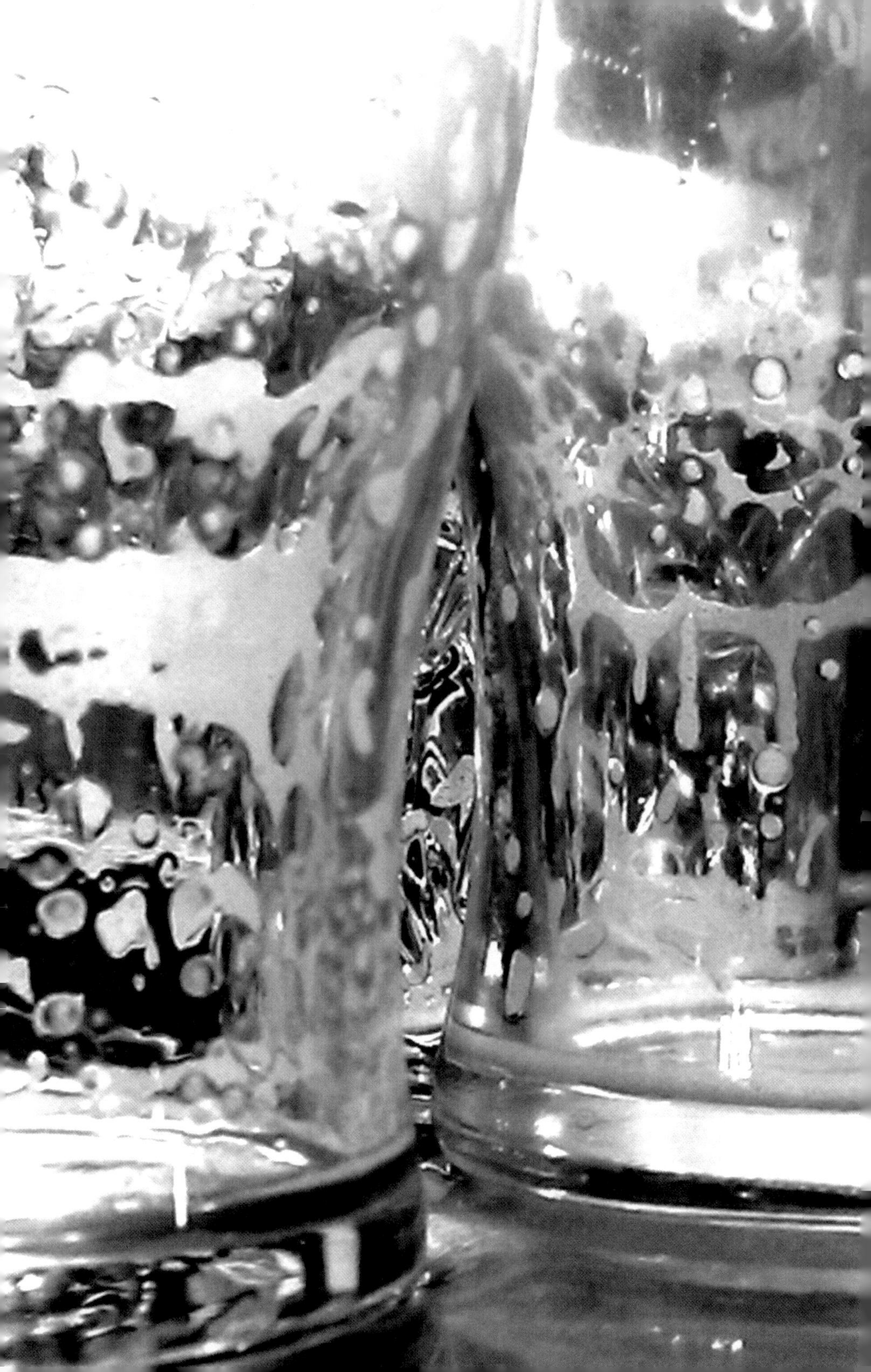

List of Beverages

BEERS, ALES AND PORTERS

Alchemy Brewery
Ritual IPA 10, 30-31

Bad Co Brewery
Wild Gravity IPA 32-33

Caledonian Brewing Company
Deuchars IPA 12

Glastonbury Microbrewery Festival Ales
Dark As Yer' At 55
Golden Chalice 54
Hedge Monkey 52
Lady of The Lake 57
Mystery Tor 56
Pilton Pop 53

Greene King / Morland Brewery
Old Speckled Hen 91

Highland Brewing Co (Swannay Brewery)
Stout 22

Homebrew
(Steve Senior) 20-21, 27

Hook Norton
Hookey Gold 87

Jennings
Cocker Hoop 92

Little Valley Brewery
Stoodley Stout 24-25

Moorhouses
Blonde Witch 8-9
Premier Bitter 29

Morland Brewery (See Green King)

Pareidolia Brewing Company
In Da Cat Pale Ale 81
Late in the Day Amber Ale 77
Pareidolia Porter 80
Pass it Down Porter 74
Pete's Peanut butter Porter 76
Right Point Red Ale 79
Sebastian Scottish Ale 75
The Duke IPA 78
YRUSO Pale Ale 82

Phoenix
Black Bee Porter 13

Saltaire Brewery
Cascade IPA 16-17, 23

Sixpoint Craft Ales
Bengali IPA 6, 18, 19, 26, 34-35, 86,95

Stewart Brewing
Pentland IPA 11, 88

Timothy Taylor
Golden Best 93
Landlord 89

The Bore
Pale Ale 15

The Hop Studio
XP 90

Unknown Brewery
Honey Porter 7

CARBONATED DRINKS

Cherry Coca-Cola 43
Coca-Cola 40, 41, 44, 45, 47, 48
Coca-Cola Life 46
Diet Coca-Cola 49
Dr Pepper 100
Vanilla Coca-Cola 42

COFFEE

Black Americano 61
Flat White 62, 64
Instant 67
Latte 60, 65, 66

LAGERS

Carlsburg 94
Corona Extra 14
Stella Artois 36-37

WHISKY

Isle of Jura 103

WINE

Côtes du Rhône 102

OTHER DRINKS

Hot Chocolate.......... 68, 69
Mocha 63
Water 98-99, 101

List of Locations

England

CUMBRIA

Arnside
The Albion Hotel 15

DERBYSHIRE

Derby
The Standing Order 94

SOMERSET

Brean
Channel View Campsite 100

Pilton
Glastonbury Festival for Contemporary Performing Arts 50-57

WEST YORKSHIRE

Halifax
Shibden Mereside Café, Shibden Park 60-61
The Big 6 32-33
The Chinese Buffet 36-37
The Percy Shaw 6,12,18,19,26,34-35,86,95
The Shears (The Paris Gates) 8-9
The Three Pigeons 13

Haworth
Haworth Old Hall Inn 92

Hebden Bridge
Organic House Café 62,63
Park Life Café 40-49, 64, 68, 69, 70
The Fox and Goose 90
The Old Gate 16-17, 23
The Trades Club 29

Sowerby Bridge
The Works 87, 89, 93

Todmorden
The Golden Lion 7

Scotland

LOTHIAN

Edinburgh
Orchard (Brae) Park 14
The Stockbridge Tap 10, 22, 30-31

MIDLOTHIAN

Penicuik
The Flotterstone Inn 11, 88

USA

FLORIDA

Sebastian
Pareidolia Brewing Company 72-82

Offshore

THE ENGLISH CHANNEL

Dover to Calais ferry
The Pride of Canterbury 98-99

ROCHDALE CANAL

Hebden Bridge
Narrowboat 20-21, 27, 91

Afore Ye Go

I hope you have enjoyed the illustrated guided tour through these surreal pages. Before we part I offer you a chance to create your own pareidolia inspired poem from the next drink you enjoy. Whether it's still or sparkling, milkshake or mocha, beer or brown ale, follow the simple instructions below, and wallow in your own creative essence.

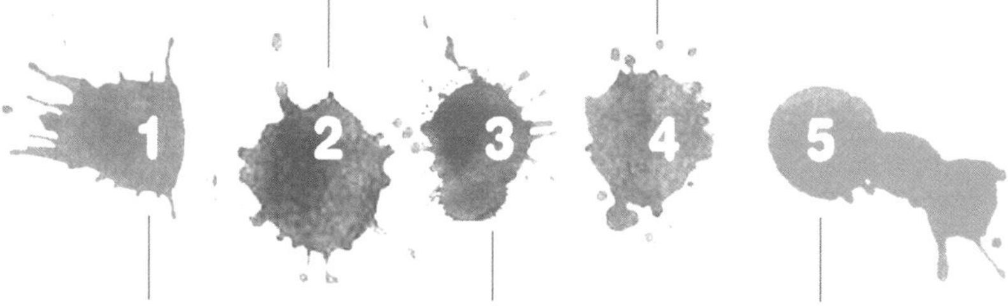

1. Have at hand a drink and a method of recording your observations (a phone, tablet, or voice recording, or altenatively, a pen, pencil, paper, or napkin).
2. For drinks that leave a pattern on the glass you can make observations after every sip, or when you have finished.
3. For fizzy drinks you will have to be very quick to see the images in the bubbles which only appear fleetingly after each pour. You can try swirling the glass to create further patterns on the sides, or look for reflections. (This method is for advanced poeteers only.)
4. Beware waiters and waitresses. They can spoil your fun.
5. Do not worry if you only see images in your drink that bear a vague resemblance to something. Tenuousness and ambiguity are your friends, embrace them.

In 1925, '*Afore ye go*' was registered as the official company slogan for Bell's Whisky. During the First World War, the Bell family would have a few cases of Bell's Extra Special Old Scotch Whisky sent down to the docks to be distributed among the troops going off to the Western Front, the idea being that they should have a wee dram '*afore ye go*'. **whiskeywise.com**

6. Write down your images as they appear.
7. People may stare. This is normal. It is only because they are jealous and because you are a more interesting person.
8. When you have had enough fun, stop.
9. Think of a hybrid title made from some of the words in your poem or inspired by them.
10. Warning, this process can become addictive. Periods of composition of more than 10 minutes without a break are ill advised.

Collaborators' Biographies

GAIA HOLMES is a West Yorkshire-born poet and a graduate of Huddersfield University where she achieved a BA in English with Creative Writing. She has previously made a living as a busker, a cleaner, a gallery attendant, an oral historian, a lollypop lady, a poet in residence at Bradford Library and Halifax festival, a freelance writer, and Creative Writing lecturer. Her debut poetry collection, *Dr. James Graham's Celestial Bed*, was published by Comma Press in 2006 and her 2nd collection, *Lifting The Piano With One Hand* was published in 2013. When not writing, Gaia tries to play the accordion with the '*Crow Hill Stompers*' band, or (wo)mans the decks as a DJ at Calderdale's local community radio station, *Phoenix FM*. (*Pages 15, 60-61*).

MAISY HOWELL is a young creative living in Somerset. She is hoping to continue her studies in drama at college and enjoys singing and playing keyboards. She also practises hula hooping and other circus skills in her holidays.
(*Pages 46, 62-63, 100*).

JASON HOWGATE was born in Dewsbury, West Yorkshire and studied fine art in Bradford and Wolverhampton. He specialises in pen and ink drawings using Rapidograph mapping pens. His artistic influences come as much from writers as visual artists and as such he has collaborated informally on a number of projects including working with Winston Plowes. (*Pages 85-95*).

LAURIE KOLP is an avid runner, lover of nature and married mother of three who enjoys living in the moment in Southeast Texas. She is the author of *Upon the Blue Couch* (Winter Goose Publishing, 2014) and *Hello It's Your Mother* (Finishing Line Press, 2015). Recent publications include the 2015 Poet's Market, *Scissors & Spackle* and the *North Dakota Quarterly*. Learn more about Laurie at lauriekolp.com
(*Pages 68-70*).

RUTH ROBSON-KING studied graphic design and typography at Jacob Kramer College of Art in her hometown of Leeds, and feels privileged to have been a student of Latvian artist, Laimonis Mierins. She moved to Notting Hill, London, soon after to pursue a freelance career with Conran, Wolff Olins, and IPC Media. Ruth also founded indie book publishing company, *Electric Press*, and has taught art to Lakota children at Pine Ridge Indian Reservation, South Dakota. She has a passion for Bauhaus inspired design, and describes herself as designer, illustrator, writer, silversmith, ornithophile, and occasional revolutionary. She shares her life with alternative arts performer husband Nik. (*Pages 65-67*).

Acknowledgements

I would like to extend a huge thank you to *Paul Silver* for his own Facebook '*coffee cup*' project, *Robin Parker* for dragons and ***The Trades Club, Hebden Bridge*** for each planting seeds of thought at the conception of this project. *Kelly* for her considered comments on format. *David Ford, Laurie Kolp* and the three H's; *Gaia Holmes, Maisy Howell*, and *Jason Howgate* for applying their poety brains to our collaborative work. *Steve Senior* and *Jason* again for their inspirational homebrew. *Charlie* and *Kim* of **The Park Life Café** for their fizzy enthusiasm and toilet gallery opportunities. *Creedy* for his relentless synchronicity. *Graham* for this elephant. *Gaia* again for her inbuilt grammar checker and pinching. *Pete Anderson* of the ***Pareidolia Brewing Company*** for embracing my madness and wholeheartedly believing that beer and poetry are a match made in heaven. My fellow found poets in the US who regularly dare to venture with me into the unknown and emerge unscathed. *Richard Hindle* at ***The Green Room Bar, Glastonbury Festival*** for inspiring refreshments. ***Wikipedia***, which never answered back when I shouted. *John Foggin* for his majestic compeering.

I also need to mention all my ***Facebook*** friends, some of whom I even know! As well as being good for finding out what people have just had for their dinner and what special accomplishments their children have recently made, if trained properly, Facebook can be an excellent resource as hopefully this book testifies. Many of the poems in **Section 1**, ***Glass Half Full,*** would not exist without it and its occupants. Namely (Alphabetically by Facebook name) [deep breath here] *Valerie Anderson Gaskill, Dave Barnes, Little Bird, Kim Lana Blackburn, Rosie Blunn, Rachel Bond, Mark Brosc Broscombe, Cathy Bryant, Tony Burger, Gillie Carpenter, Charlie Carr, Valerie Chapman, Julie Rose Clark, David Clegg, Rose Condo, Mark Connors, Ben Cornish, Katherine Coussement, Joanna Crosby, Deborah Cunliffe, Skye Darkwoods, Sebastian Degorce, Sarah L. Dixon, Rose Drew, Steve Ely, Petrova C. Fairhurst, Louise Fazackerley, Max Ferrari, Steve Fiddle, Helen Fitt, David Ford, Diana Forrest, Catherine Gaboreau, Daniel Galef, Jennifer Gaye Gardner, Rachel Geldard, Julia Gray, Aylin Erengül Gregg, Tudor Gwynn, Tony Halsall, Catherine Heartfield, Derek Heine, Keiron Higgins, Peppy Hills, Tess Hills, Linda Hodges, Gaia Holmes, Bob Horne, Maisy Howell, Sarah Jackson, David Jarman, Dave Jellybean, Clare Johnston, Mab Jones, Cat Kinson, Justine Knight, Andrew Lawson, Martin Long, John Lusardi, Connor MacLeod, Andrew Marsh, Rachel McGladdery, George McKim, Jos Murphy, Steve Nash, Matthew Nicholson, Elly O'Grady, Michaela O'Sullivan, Marion Oxley, Lazlo Palko, Freddie Philips, Louella Ramsden, Colin Robinson, Sara Robinson, Nik Robot-King (who also worked on the final edit), Carol Robson, Julie Rose-Clark, Christina Rothenbeck, Laura Rzhepishevska, Su Senior, Andy Smith, Sheila Sondik, Wayneo Martyn Stankiewicz, Caroline Sturges, Ric Taylor, James Telfor, William Thirsk-Gaskill, Kath Thorpe, Brian Toberman, Robin Turner, Nicky Vaux, Clare Wakefield, Steven Waling, Genevieve L. Walsh, Liz Wells, Jax Westmoreland, Joe Williams* and finally now we have arrived at the other end of the alphabet, the speed skating milkman himself, *Mr Terry Woodward.*

Actually not quite finally as there needs to be a special place here for the arrival of three exceptional people, firstly my editor, and percolator of dreams, *Ruth 'Hawkeye'*, and the irrepressible *Ross Kightly*, who, by grasping the nettle of tedium that proof reading can sometimes be, made this a better book. And thirdly, the unclassifiable *Angus Barclay*, who appeared serendipitously at the very end of this project. A position befitting his special talents as an indexer of books.

If any of you see me and can catch me, it's my round,

Winston Plowes

(Beer Poeteer).

Further Reading

Manifestoes of Surrealism
by Andre Breton. Translated by Richard Seaver and Helen R. Lane
The University of Michigan Press, New edition. 1972

Maldoror and Poems
by Alastair Brotchie. Edited by Mel Gooding
Penguin Classics, Reprinted. 1978

A Book of Surrealist Games
by Alastair Brotchie. Edited by Mel Gooding
Shambhala Publications Inc, 1995

Surrealist Poetry in English
by Edward B. Germain
Penguin Modern Classics, 1978

Masters of Deception: Escher, Dali and the Artists of Optical Illusion
by Douglas R. Hofstadter and Al Seckel
Sterling, 2007

Another World: Dali, Magritte, Miro and the Surrealists
by Patrick Elliott
Trustees of the National Galleries of Scotland, 2010

Dada and Surrealism
by Robert Short
Laurence King Publishing, 1994

The Redstone Inkblot Test
ANON.
Redstone Press, 2003

Experiential foundations of Rorschach's test
(Studies in existentialism and phenomenology)
by Ernest G. Schachtel
Tavistock Publications, 1967

Camouflage and Mimicry
by Denis Owen
Oxford University Press, 1980

An Atom of Meaning: Playing with Pareidolia:
Accidental Art for People who Can't Draw
by Frances Culshaw
Momerath publishing, 2013

The Princeton Encyclopedia of Poetry and Poetics: Fourth Edition
by Roland Greene and Stephen Cushman
Princeton University Press, 2012

Hamlet
by William Shakespeare and Cedric Watts
Wordsworth Editions, paperback ed, Annotated ed, 1992

Index

A

Aboriginal art 91
Adams, Ansel 25, 109
aeroplane fuselage 48
air bags 46
Albion Hotel (Arnside) 15
aliens 25, 37, 86, 89, 98,100, 101
Alium ursinum 103, 116
alligators 31, 35
amoebas 25, 109
Anderson, Pete 73
Angmar, Witch Lord of 54, 112
Ant Hill Mob's car 44, 111
anteaters 7, 81
anticyclone 42, 111
antlers 22
anvil 21
apophenia 1
archerfish 89, 114
architectural features 45, 111
atomic bomb 37, 56, 110
automatism/automatic writing 2
autumn 67
Ayres Rock 6, 107

B

Back to the Future 9, 107
Baileys Irish Cream 80, 114
Baily's beads 42, 111
balloons 40, 66, 89
balls 45
Barbapapa 98, 116
barbed wire 15
BASE jumper 8, 114
basketball player 31
bat-signal 46, 111
Batman 7, 107
Batty, Nora 25, 109
bear, headless 62
beard, iron filing 40
bee, exploding 62
bee monsters (Dr Who) 11, 108
Beelzeboul 87, 114
beer *see* specific beers
bell 98
Bengali IPA (Sixpoint Craft Ales) 6, 18, 19, 26, 34–35, 86, 95
Berk (Trapdoor character) 23, 109
Bibendum 40, 111
bicycles 22
- front derailleur 94, 115

Big Six (Halifax) 32–33
birds 27, 63, 78, 98, 101, 110
bison 33
Black Bee Porter (Phoenix) 13
Blobby, Mr 17, 108
Blonde Witch (beer) 9
blood 102
body parts 14, 31, 54, 60, 98, 104
bones 9, 56, 88, 98
boomerangs 7, 43, 107
boots 13, 29
Bore Pale Ale 15
bracelet 47, 111
Brain Dots (puzzle app) 23, 109
breasts 10
see also nipples
bridal bouquet 42
broad beans 49
Brooker, Alex 37, 110
Brown House-moth (*Hofmannophila pseudospretella*) 102, 116
bubble blower 66
bubble gum 46
Buddhist temple 87
bulls 17, 31, 33
butterflies 65, 93
buttocks 10

C

cakes 45, 79
calabash pipe 76, 113
camels 68, 105
canal 65
Carlsberg 94
cars
- brake disks 91
- engines 78
- steering wheels 37, 82
- windscreen 68

Cascade IPA (Saltaire Brewery) 16–17, 23
cashmere 13, 108
cathedral buttresses 45, 111
Catpone, Al 9, 107
cats 63
- kissing 1, 6
- space 89

cave drawings 91
Ceiling Demons (band) 9, 108
chain links 21
chairs 57
chakras 14, 108
cherub 23, 54
chess players 11
chicks 21, 91
Chinese Buffet (Halifax) 36–37
chocolate kisses 53, 112
Churn Milk Joan 94, 115
circus performers 31
Clangers 81, 114
clothing 65, 75, 81, 91, 98
clouds 33, 44, 48, 63, 80, 82, 111
Clouseau, Inspector 9
clown 98
CND symbol 98, 116
coalbunker 67
Coca-Cola glasses 2, 38, 39–49
Cocker Hoop (Jennings) 92
Coffee
- Americano 61
- beans 65, 66
- cups, found 2, 58-71
- flat white 62-64
- granules 67
- Latte 60, 65
- Milky 19
- Mocha 63

compass needle 81
conga eel 23, 109
Cookie Monster 81, 114
coral reef 67
cormorant (*Phalacrocorax carbo*) 101, 116
Corona Extra Lager 14
Côtes du Rhône 102
cows 31, 77, 113
- jumping over moon 18, 109
- tongue of 94
- udders of 6

Coyote, Wile E. 95, 116
crabs 37, 100
craters 19, 60
creatures, unknown 53, 81
Cretan bull 17, 108
crocodiles 33, 35, 88, 114
croctopus 80, 113
crowd-sourcing 2
Crunchie Bar 21, 109
Cthulhu 17, 31, 108

cucumber 66
cul-de-sac 42, 111
curling stones 12, 108
curtains 43, 48

D

Dali, Salvador 2
dancers 15, 17, 31, 62, 80, 98
Dark As Yer 'At (Glastonbury Microbrewery) 55
deep-sea diver's helmet 6
Deuchars IPA (Caledonian Brewing Company) 12
diamonds 41, 100
diver 22
dog chew 60
dogs 25, 31, 33, 65, 68, 75
- balloon 89
- dancing 62
dolphin 31
door, magic 82
Dover to Calais ferry 98–99
Dr Pepper 100
Dr Who 11, 31, 87, 116
dragons 5, 17, 29, 33, 35, 53
- Chinese 61, 112
dreams 65, 103
driftwood 81
ducks 14, 35
- rubber 90
Duke IPA (Pareidolia Brewing Company) 78

E

Earth, from space 76, 95
Ecce homo 17, 108
Echo 90
eclipse 89
eel 23
eggs 31
- fried 37
Eiger, North Face of 82, 114
Elephant Man 31, 110
elephants 9, 27, 74
- toy 68
embryo/foetus 19, 104
emergency button, underwater 37
emus 7
Endor 33, 110
engagement ring 94
engine 78
Eskimos 90
Eternal Wave 25
Everest, Mount 60, 112
Ewok 31, 110
Eye of Sauron 100, 116
eyebrow 49
eyes 45, 61, 70, 94, 100

F

Facebook 2, 5, 101
faces 9, 15, 18, 49, 53, 54, 65
- angry 23
- of animals 55, 78, 80
- evil 22
- ghost 46
- masked 75
- shocked 102
- smiling 55
fallopian tubes 60
figures 42, 56, 63, 65, 91, 103
- lonely 86
- religious 92
- running 25
- scratching head 60
- skipping, with enormous hole in torso 80
- stooping 75
- waving 102
- on a wheel 98
fire 67
fish 9, 17, 35, 37, 87, 88, 89, 98, 100, 101, 114
fishing/fishermen 7, 98
flags 44
flamenco dancers 17, 31, 108
Flintstone, Wilma 49, 111
floorboards 102
Florida (US) 2, 73
Flotterstone Inn (Penicuik, Midlothian) 11, 88
flowers 14, 43, 87, 88, 89
fluorescent lights 23, 49
flux capacitor 9, 107
foetus/embryo 19, 104
footballer 13
footprints 55, 66, 104
Fox and Goose (Hebden Bridge) 90
foxes 11, 25, 35, 52
Frankenstein 86, 114
Friesian cow 77, 113
Froglets 53, 112
frogs 33, 98, 101
- eggs of 100
froth/foam 5, 98–99
fruit/vegetables 41, 100, 102, 104

G

galaxies/nebulae 61, 78, 112, 113
gazelle 56
geese in flight 94
geometric shapes 98, 99, 100
Germain, Edward B. 3
geyser, mud 14
ghetto blaster 12, 108
ghosts 9, 17, 25, 31, 33, 37, 46, 80
- encountered by camel 68
giraffe 11
Gitanes 92, 115
Glastonbury Festival 2, 51-57
goat wattles 23, 109
Gobi Desert 18, 109
goblin 22
gold, panning for 64
Golden Chalice (Glastonbury Microbrewery) 54
Golden Lion (Todmorden) 7
Gooding, Mel 3
Great Bear (constellation) 54, 112
Green Room Bar (Glastonbury Festival) 51
Grimm's fairytale 61, 112
guitars 63
guns 48, 63, 90, 115
Gypsy tart 18, 109

H

hair 16, 19, 29, 40, 49, 78, 103
halo 41
halva 44, 111
Hamlet (Shakespeare) 105
hammerhead shark 29
hand shadows 22, 88
hands 21, 31, 40, 104
hanglider 74
harbour 77
hares 37, 60, 62
Hasselhoff, David 64, 112
hats 14, 46, 80, 89, 104, 114
Hawksclough Bridge (Mytholmroyd) 93
Haworth Old Hall Inn (Haworth) 92
headband 74
headphones 40
Heath Robinson contraptions 90, 115
Hedge Monkey (Glastonbury Microbrewery) 52
hedgerows 61, 87

henge 15, 108
Hiroshima 37, 110
Hockney, David 88, 114
Hofmannophila pseudospretella 102, 116
Holmes, Gaia 15, 60-61, 122
homebrew 20–21, 27
honey porter 7
Hookey Gold (Hook Norton) 87
hope, ray of 82
Hopeful Monsters (album) 82, 114
horseshoe 100
horses 6, 17, 29, 33, 43
- White Horse of Uffington 79, 113
hot chocolate 18, 68, 69
Howell, Maisy 42,62-63,100, 122
Howgate, Jason 85, 122
Hula hoops 43
hurricanes 45

I

ibex 37, 110
ice cream cone 74
ice hockey mask 41
ice sheets/flow 63, 86
In Da Cat Pale Ale (Pareidolia Brewing Company) 81
inkblot tests 3
Italy 25

J

jalapeño pepper 76, 113
jalebi 92, 115
jazz musician 31
jellyfish 1, 17, 25, 29, 37, 40
jester 23
join the dots 93
juggling 86, 114
Jura malt whiskey 103

K

K-9 (Dr Who) 94, 116
kangaroo 48
- dart-throwing 104
Kateroo 7, 107
Katia, Hurricane 45
kidney 98
kiwi (bird) 7, 11, 22, 82, 107
Kolp, Laurie 68-70, 122
Krueger, Freddy 9, 108

L

lace, Belgian 5
Lady of the Lake (Glastonbury Microbrewery) 56
lambs 33
lamp, Aladdin style 64
lamp lighter 66
lampshade 47
Landlord (Timothy Taylor) 89
landscapes 15, 18, 19, 23, 31, 69
- on fire 67
- trees/hedgerows in 60, 61
Late in the Day Amber Ale (Pareidolia Brewing Company) 77
lathe swarfe 78, 113
letters of the alphabet 11, 47, 77, 98, 111
lichens 92, 115
lights 23, 49, 64, 102
likenesses 1–2
- typology of 1
lions 7, 87
lips 21
- fat 75
- scabby 63
lizard 17
Loch Ness monster 35, 110
love hearts 1, 7, 21, 25, 44, 63, 87, 98
lung 14

M

magpie 29
Manning, Bernard 37, 110
manta ray (*M. birostris/M. alfredi*) 101, 116
maps/country outlines 33, 42, 43, 46, 49, 98, 100, 110
marshmallow 19
martini glass 74
mash tun 76, 77
Master and Margarita (Bulgakov) 87, 114
Matisse, Henri-Émile-Benoît 8–9, 31, 107
mermaids 31, 61, 62
meteor showers 91, 115
'Mice' (online game) 46
Mickey Mouse 17, 108
Milky Way 40, 111
Miró, Joan 25, 109
mist 54
Moby Dick 49, 90, 111, 115
mole, stuck in drainpipe 95
monkeys 18, 22, 78, 80, 109
monsters 82, 86
moon 26, 37
- crescent 44, 45, 48
- man on the 66
- surface of/craters on 60, 63
moon buggy 78, 113
Moore, Henry Spencer 1, 13, 108
Moorehouses Premier Bitter 28–29
Morrissey 31
mould 18, 66
mountains 25, 26, 69, 74, 88, 93, 94
- Eiger 82, 114
- Everest 60, 112
- Rushmore 55, 112
moustaches 56, 65
- handlebar 22, 109
mouths 10
see also lips; teeth
mushroom 42
musical notation 80
mustard pot 74
Mystery Tor (Glastonbury Microbrewery) 56

N

nebulae *see* galaxies/nebulae
necklace 66
net being cast 98, 99
New Zealand 14
nipples 37
Nod, Land of 90, 115
Noddy 75, 113
nose 79
- bloody 65
- running 77
notebook, spiral-bound 21
numbers 48
nutcrackers 35

O

ocean liners 90
octo-goat 31
octopus 9, 92
oil wheel projections 91, 104, 115
Old Gate (Hebden Bridge) 17, 23
Old Grey Whistle Test 79, 113
Old Mother Shipton 88
Old Speckled Hen (Greene King/ Morland Browory) 91
organ pipes 64

Organic House Café
(Hebden Bridge) 62, 63
Orion (constellation) 43, 111
Orkney Stout
(Highland Brewing Co.) 22
oystercatcher 27, 110

P

Pac-Man 9, 29, 98, 99, 107
paint splatter 89
pandas 31, 75
paper bag 21
parachutist 82
paranoiac critical technique 2
pareidolia 1, 2, 97
Pareidolia Brewing Company 73–83
Pareidolia Porter
(Pareidolia Brewing Company) 80
Park Life Café (Hebden Bridge)
38-49, 68, 69, 70-71
Pass it Down Porter
(Pareidolia Brewing Company) 74
patternicity/pattern-seeking 1, 2
paw prints 18, 77
Peanut Butter Porter
(Pareidolia Brewing Company) 76
Peloton d'exécution 68, 113
pelvis 9
penguin 19
Pentland IPA
(Stewart Brewing) 11, 88
Peppa Pig 37, 111
Pequod, The 49, 111
Percy Shaw (Halifax)
6, 12, 18, 19, 26, 34–35, 95
petrol pumps 53
Phalacrocorax carbo 101, 116
pianist 12
pig 37
pike 35
Pilton Pop
(Glastonbury Microbrewery) 53
pinball machine 76, 113
Pinocchio 25, 109
pitcher plant 81, 114
planets 70, 76
plastic glasses 51
Playboy Bunny 9
plughole 26
poetry, process of creating 1–3
- and Surrealism 2, 3
pop art 87, 114
popcorn 100
pork chop 41
porthole 78
praying/gesticulating figure 21
Presley, Elvis 17, 108
propeller 47, 111
Psycho (film) 92, 115
puffer fish 87
Punch & Judy 9, 107
punk rocker 9
puppets 95

Q

question mark 56

R

rabbits 23, 60, 76, 77
- astride rocking horse 75
- with club 87
rain dance 15, 108
rainbow 57
ram's horns/head 45, 98, 100
ramsons (*Alium ursinum*) 103, 116
razor, electric 14
Read, Herbert 3
religious figures 92
Rhincodon typus 100, 116
rhinoceros 60
Right Point Red Ale
(Pareidolia Brewing Company) 79
Ritual IPA
(Alchemy Brewery) 10, 30–31
Robson-King, Ruth 65-67, 122
rockets 25, 40
Romanesque style 92, 115
Roobarb 35, 110
Rorschach Test 3
rubber duck 90
rug, bearskin 22
Rushmore, Mount 55, 112

S

Saint Bernard dogs 62, 75, 112
sand 26, 45
sandpiper 27, 110
Sauron, eye of 100, 116
saxophone 53
Scarfe, Gerald 57, 112
Scooby-Doo ghosts 17, 33, 108
Scortino, Jim 73
Scotland 31, 113
Scream, The (Munch) 19, 61, 109
scrimshaw 90, 115
sculpture 1, 13, 112
sea/ocean 37, 95
- ice in 63, 86
- images of foam in 98–99
seagulls 27, 78
seahorse 11
seals 61
seashore 26, 93, 115
seaweed 14
Sebastian Scottish Ale
(Pareidolia Brewing Company) 75
seed germinating 95
Senior, Steve
(home brewer) 20–21, 27
seventh wave 76, 113
Shakespeare, William 2, 105
sharks 37
- fin of 13
- hammerhead 29
- whale 100, 116
Shears
(aka Paris Gates, Halifax) 9
sheep 33
shellfish 26, 31
Shibden Mereside Café (Halifax)
60, 61
shrimp, mantis 31
sideburns 44, 111
signs/symbols
7, 17, 42, 45, 86, 98, 116
Simpsons, The 31, 55, 110
simulacrum/simulacra 1
skiers 94
skies 41
- constellations in 43, 54
- vapour trails in 47
skulls 33, 56, 76, 92
slime mold 66, 113
Slimer (Ghostbusters character)
37, 110
sloth (animal) 86
slug 17
sluice gates 103
snakes 55, 79
Snoopy 17, 108
snow 54, 68, 93, 113
- angels 102, 116
- snowflakes 13
socks 42, 69, 113
solar flares 13, 67, 86, 95, 108

space phenomena
25, 37, 70, 76, 86, 102, 103
- Baily's beads 42, 111
- constellations 43, 54, 112
- galaxies/nebulae 61, 78, 112, 113
- meteor showers 91, 115
spacecraft 86, 93, 101, 115
spade 77
sparks 48
sperm 88, 95
spider monkeys 22, 109
Spider-Man 79, 113
spiders 46, 89, 100
'Splash' (Hockney) 88, 114
SpongeBob Squarepants 31, 110
squid 46
stag beetles 33, 37, 110
Standing Order (Derby) 94
Star Trek characters 13, 108
Star Trek transporter 76, 113
Star Wars characters
31, 33, 98, 110, 116
starfish 44
stars 43, 54
steering wheels 37, 82
Stella Artois 36–37
Stockbridge Tap (Edinburgh)
10, 22, 30–31
stone wall 35
Stoodley Stout (Little Valley) 24–25
storms 45, 67, 70, 111
stormtroopers (Star Wars) 33, 110
submarines 64, 93, 112, 115
sugar mouse 69
sunglasses, Oakley 7, 107
Super Mario 42, 111
superlambanana, elongated 11, 108
Surrealism 2, 3
Sustrans waymarker 7, 107
swarfe 78, 113
swimmers 35, 63
swimming goggles 92
synchronicity 1

T

tadpoles 100, 104
teapots 47, 62, 64, 103
Teenage Mutant Ninja Turtles
101, 116
teeth 10, 75, 87
telephones 1, 11, 18, 41, 98
tennis player 53
tent 88
Thing, The 100, 116
thistle heads 6
Three Pigeons (Halifax) 13
tiger stripes 57
Tintin's rocket 25, 109
toad spawn 77
toilet scum 92
Trades Club 29
traffic lights 102
trains 62, 80, 102
Trapdoor (TV series) 23, 109
Traveler, The 13, 108
treasure map 31
trees 41, 60, 77, 94, 95, 116
twins, conjoined 26, 109
tyre marks 91

U

U-boat 64, 112
Uffington White Horse 79
ultrasound scan, inconclusive 47
unicorn 17, 108

V

vapour trails 47
verdigris 82, 114
vinyl record 66, 112
volcano 26
Volleyball, game of 62, 91

W

Watcher in the Water 79, 113
water boatman 66, 113
water sprites 95
Wazowski, Mike 100, 116
weasel 105
whale shark
(*Rhincodon typus*) 100, 116
whale sperm 88
whales 1, 17, 61, 95, 105
- jumping over moon 37
- swallowing ball 104
Whernside 23, 109
whisky 103
White House, The 18, 109
white noise 94
Wild Gravity IPA
(Bad Co Brewery) 32–33
will-o'-the-wisps 26, 109
Willy Wisp 6, 107
Wilson, Keppel and Betty 91, 115
wind 49
- cherub 23, 109
windows 23, 43, 45
wine 102
wolf 25, 46, 55
Works, The (Sowerby Bridge)
25, 87, 89, 93
wrestlers 9
writing 35
- Arabic 44
- mirror 49, 89

X

XP (Hop Studio) 90

Y

Y-Fronts 82
YRUSO Pale Ale
(Pareidolia Brewing Company)
82–83

Z

zebra 31
Zig and Zag 9, 107
Zygons 87, 114

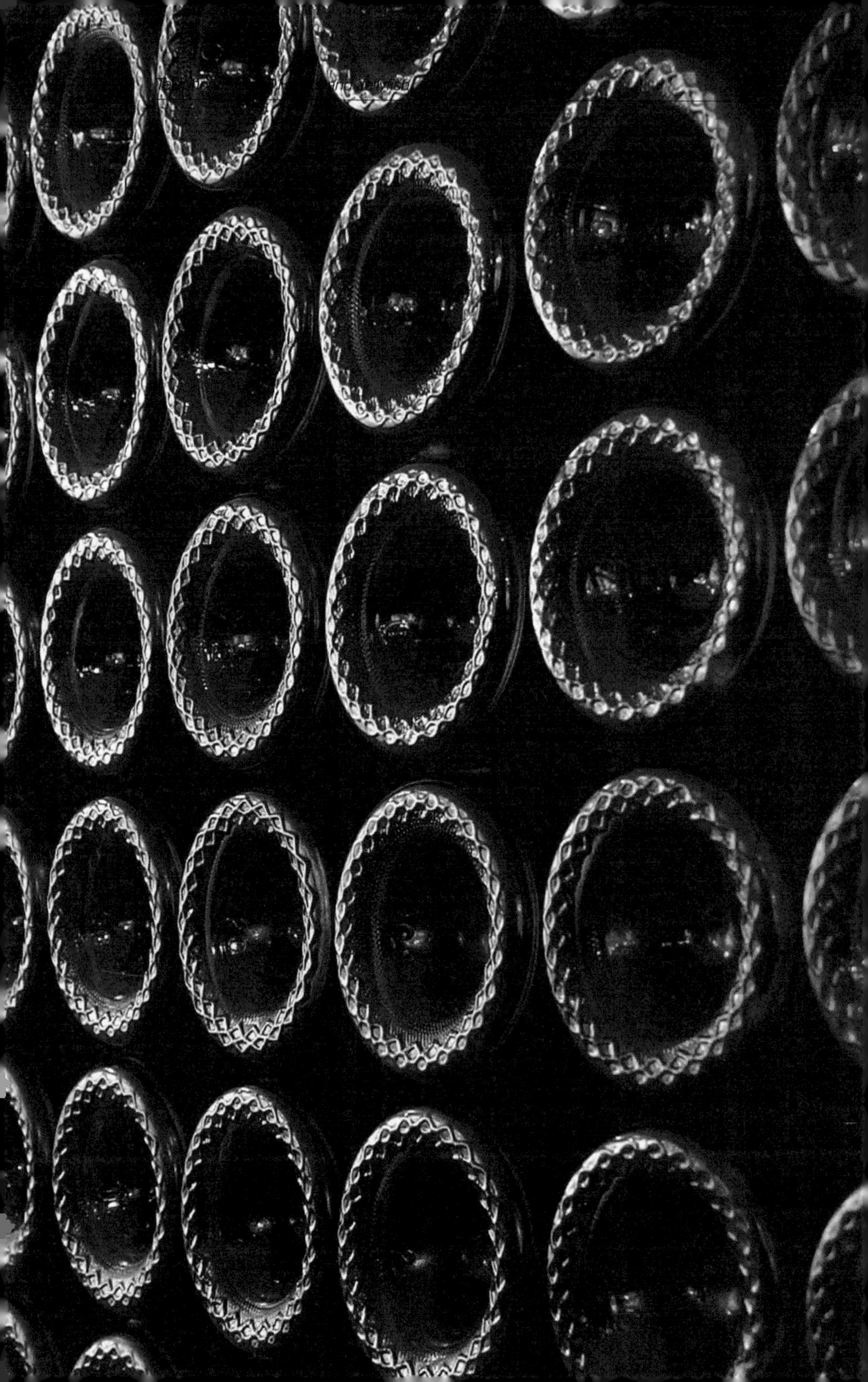